SHINY CARPET

Christian McAvoy

Raider Publishing International

New York　　　London　　　Cape Town

Published By Raider Publishing International
www.RaiderPublishing.com
New York London Cape Town
Printed in the United States of America and the United Kingdom

Dedication

I DEDICATE THIS BOOK TO MY SON, HARRY. I WAS THERE on the day he was born. Of course, I was an absolute wreck, but I still managed to cut the umbilical cord. I know that it was the greatest day of my life. He has brought me nothing but happiness since that day, and I hope until the day I die, whenever that may be. I truly hope there will be lots of years spent with him and hope he thinks enough of me to spend those years with me. I love him dearly and have no idea how my life would be now without him. Ella, for undying support in everything I do and her love without compromise. Thanks, Harry and Ella. Your loving father

This book is also dedicated to my teachers from Dixon Road School— Mr. Scott, Miss. Peal, Mr. Frankombe and others such as Mr. Evans, Mr. Barber and, of course, Mr. Jarvis, whose early guidance and support saved my life. To the people who over the years have badgered me into writing this— without them, I wouldn't have journeyed on this road. My thanks also go to Paul Titley who has given me some honest feedback in the progress of this book, which has been invaluable, if not brutal. To Simon Wain, whose energy pushed me forward.

To my best friend, Mark Hart— the only person who tried to understand me, and the only person who, frankly, wanted to. I owe a great debt to Mark for keeping me close to the ground for the last thirty years. Without you, mate, God knows where I would be now.

You have been a real rock and I applaud you and wish I

could be half the man you are. If I could aspire to that, it would be enough. You humble gentleman.

To Will Hart, for the great BBQ'S and for again being an inspiration. When God made you he broke the mould. He had to, it was to big to carry. Thanks for your patience over the years. I realise I have not been easy and promise to replace the the pickled gerkins of which I am sure has sprouted to a fine tree in May Lane.

To Lenny Killeen for bouncing stories off and for listening— cheers, mate. We have laughed and cried, haven't we, bud? Although I was 22nd choice for your best man behind the guy at co-op in the pizza department and the lady who tends the graves at Svalöv church I did my best and felt needed. Thanks mate.

To Matty for educating me in English. Like pronouncing 'barth' instead of 'bath'. Breathtaking. And to Paddy for his support and kindness over the years.

Mostly this book has to be dedicated to Frank Delaney and children just like him. The forgotten child who has never left me for one day. I really hope that he reads it and makes contact. If only to let me know he is still alive.

Foreword

THIS IS A TRUE STORY OF MY CHILDHOOD IN THE INNER CITY of Birmingham. The story takes place between the ages of six and thirteen. Just a seven-year span, but the events therein would affect me for the rest of my life in some shape or form. Normality within something abnormal. Violence; abuse; poverty. All normal, everyday occurrences, yet totally avoidable. In my circumstances, anyway.

I was born in Marston Green Hospital, Birmingham, on January 17, 1966. My mom recently told me that I was a pain in the ass back then, and remained one. I was the third of four children to Mr. and Mrs. James McAvoy, Irish Catholic. My dad was from Belfast, and my mom from Dublin. They met in Birmingham, England, on a sunny Sunday afternoon outside a jewellery shop. My dad had just left the navy, and was in accommodation. He was one of the lucky ones. He had found it particularly difficult to be accepted in any accommodation, as in those days they were very picky. I think it was his Hollywood good looks that swayed it for him. He told me that one sign actually said, 'no blacks, no dogs and no Irish'. The Irish were actually less favourable than dogs as tenants in those days.

My mom was seventeen, and my dad was twenty-one. It was 1957, and love felt the same. After a year of courting, they were married. My dad then joined the army, and made his way to serving as corporal in the Royal Hussars. He was discharged with ill health, eight and a half years later— an ulcer in his stomach. The army medical team had taken away half of his stomach before they discharged him.

They travelled extensively during that time. My mother had followed him to Singapore— where my oldest brother, Seamus, was born— and to other places, and finally to Germany, where my sister, Martha, was born two years later, and I five years after that. My younger brother, Robert, was born five years after me in the same hospital, prematurely. My earliest recollection from that time is when I was driving with my dad in a Morris Minor traveller, leant from Ron, my dad's friend, and going to see my mom and Robbie. He was hooked up to a machine with what seemed like a thousand tubes sticking out of him. Small like a doll. It didn't seem real. Life— so fragile, yet so strong.

What was this little thing getting himself into? Let me tell you.

This is Mom and Dad in Germany, with a neighbour's daughter

Author's notes

THE NAMES HAVE BEEN CHANGED, ALTHOUGH I DON'T think they need to be protected. They might think otherwise. Some of the names have been changed also to protect the integrity of the story.

Stories are told throughout the book as they come into my head. Not in any specific order, but as I remember them. I will also drift from time to time from one story to another, so pay attention.

If the story portrays any member of the family in a bad way, I must apologise for that. My father was a sick man and got through his illness in the only way he knew how. He did his best. The best he could physically, emotionally and mentally. When my father was well, he was a loving, caring, affectionate, charming, intelligent man who embraced his family and his family duties as every father should. However, when his illness took over, it became too much for him and he struggled in vain. Do not look upon him as a useless man dependent on drugs, but rather as a man with a sickness. He too was a victim of circumstance.

My mother had to cope in the most strenuous of circumstances, and was under an enormous amount of pressure. I understand that now, but at the time I thought that she just didn't care. That is not true. She was caught up in a circle of good and very bad times with someone she loved dearly, and after fifty-two years they are still together and are still the best of friends— a true testament to the power of love and understanding. I applaud this.

I look back and think that he could have done so much better. That is, of course, looking at it with a perception as to how I would have handled it. That is not reality. It was not me who was sick, trying to bring up four kids. Escapism on the dark days was the only thing my father had. That became the reality of every day. He spent most of his waking hours in emotional pain and it was a constant battle for him to get up and live a normal life. He did his

v

best. He loved me, and my mother loved me. I know that. I definitely had that. As a parent I now realise that all you can do is your best, but never fail to show them love, compassion and understanding. I just hope it's enough for my child. Or he might be writing a book about his childhood in much the same vain. I hope that will not be the case.

My older brother was also trying to deal with the same problems I had on a daily basis and therefore I received a lot of his anger and frustrations. Seamus has come to terms with those problems and has become very successful in his chosen career. The fact that he was also coming to terms with his sexuality, at a very early age, in a catholic environment did not help my situation either. I have brushed the subject with humour as I have with most things in my life. This is not meant to offend anyone and if it does then please forgive me.

All my life I have dealt with things in one way. Humour. It is defence mechanism and is not meant to offend. The fact that he is Gay doesn't matter one jot. I do not care what sexuality he is. It has nothing to do with me. I think there is way to much emphasis thrust upon this subject. If people Could just live, love and be loved, regardless of race, colour, creed or sexual preference, the world would be a brighter, kinder place. I will always love my brother and the rest of my family regardless of the circumstances.

I must also state that above all I loved my parents and still do.

SHINY CARPET

Christian McAvoy

Contents

1

The McAvoys, and So Close, Yet So Far

MY OLDER BROTHER, SEAMUS, WAS ALWAYS A BIT different but whatever happened in a big fight, we backed each other up. He could always look after himself, but, to be honest, he never had a chance. We were probably the poorest of all the families in the grove and weren't exactly hip, if you know what I mean. Then, when Paul Williams shot an arrow into Seamus' face and he became blind in one eye, it all started to go downhill for him. Peters and Lee were cool on the telly, but, in reality, Seamus had a big afro and had great suntans in the summer. So I called him 'Stevie Wonder' with his glasses on and 'cock-eyed' when he took his glasses off.

He did not have a lot of luck when he was growing up. We really didn't think it could get much worse until he was dragged half a kilometre by a double-decker bus. Would you know, he was around at the back of the bus holding the bar and swinging out whilst the bus was going along, and the only reason he didn't lose a leg was the platform shoes he was wearing. Which he detested. He was showing off in front of a girl, shouting, "Look at me; look at me."

His flares— which had been blowing in the wind— had got caught in the nuts of the rear wheel and dragged him in.

1

In truth, there was enough cloth in those Oxford bags to clothe a small village in Peru. It's no wonder he nearly died that day. He was going to go one way or the other. My money was on the human kite. I honestly thought, tell a lie, was hoping, he was going to take off and his flares would fold up like a badly packed parachute and plummet to the ground.

I think it was Kevin O'Hara who came to the house and said that Seamus had been knocked down by a bus. I must admit I did laugh a bit to begin with and I'm going to tell you why. Every morning, as long as I could remember, I was awoken not by the soft whisperings of a loving mom with a cup of drinking chocolate, but by a wedged shoe high on the forehead at fifty kilometres an hour or a knuckle sandwich at the same speed. The day would then proceed in the same vain and end up with Seamus trying to dislocate my knees and trying to twist my arms so far up my back I could easily reach back into my pockets. Forgive me for wanting him dead. So to hear that the person responsible might get his just deserts, at last, filled me with a happiness that came out as a howling laugh. Almost like a banshee. For the first time in my life I actually thought I might come out on top. His squashed body would be my exit to a new life. A life with hopes and dreams. This was my chance at something good.

I was delighted. I ran down to the bus, looking for the mangled corpse. There were people everywhere. Police, fire engines and, of course, the usual crowd looking for the bits and pieces— remembering what they had seen so they could re-tell the whole morbid story to their families over tea that night. I pushed my way through the crowd and then realised my worst fears were indeed correct. He was alive. The tears reached me quickly, and everybody thought that I was sad. Kevin, who had given me the original news, had followed me back to the scene and rushed to my side.

Shiny Carpet 3

He said, "It's okay, mate, he's going be okay."
I was in shock. I couldn't really say much. So close, yet so far. Just my bloody luck. Two separate incidents: an arrow, five millimetres from his brain, which would have meant instant death; a double-decker bus that weighed thirty tons, fully loaded, runs over him. He survives both instances, and will eventually come out smiling. *I will never*, I thought, *have other chances like these. Never.* I would have to endure this sadistic bastard for the rest of my life. I think this is where my love for different cultures actually began. The bus driver was an Indian. He looked at me quite strangely and thought I was being sarcastic when I said to him 'better luck next time'. I wasn't being sarcastic when I also told him it was a good effort, though.

The next thing I remember was being pulled out of the driver's seat of the bus. I would have run over him again, I swear. In the police car, everybody thought I was in shock and believed the story that I was going to push it into reverse. Maybe that was the case. I could reverse it back up the hill and hit the throttle.

I could see the headlines in the paper the next day: 'Orphan Annie lookalike kills brother and forty spectators in bus horror. Police said he was laughing all the way into the crowd and beyond'.

It would be great reading. I could spend the next fifteen to twenty in prison with three square meals a day and just make sure I didn't, under any circumstances, drop the soap.

No it wasn't to be. He would survive this and every other attempt on his life. They could never prove anything. Not enough evidence.

A day trip out to Cannon Hill Park. We went there occasionally with my Auntie Helen and her children. From Left: Kevin, Christian, Seamus, Martha, Martin and Michael. My Auntie Helen bought the ice creams. She had a car, too.

Seamus never played football before the tragic accident that nearly cost him his life. Tragic. Tragic. The lucky bastard. He wasn't really one for team sports. Well, anything that required masculinity.

Tongues begin to wag. It was a hot summer. No, not really.

"Is Seamus gay?" they were asking.

Well, actually, they weren't nearly as polite as they are today.

"Is Seamus a puff?" they actually asked.

It didn't matter to me then, and it doesn't matter to me now. I hated him then. I hate him…

He didn't play football, loved tennis, and his favourite singer was Barbara Streisand. It was all beginning to make sense. I don't know who noticed it first— me or the puff next door. Oh the shame of it. Kevin O'Hara's older brother was the stud of the Grove. Robbie Maloney's older brother was the tough nut of the Grove. My older brother, in the meantime, was miming to Barry Gibb whilst whitening his tennis pumps.

What the hell was I going to do with a sadist Liberace? Hoped the piano fell on him? It was, indeed, my only hope.

The bus incident wasn't the only time he nearly died. I attempted a few others.

I remember him showing off in his roller skates on the top of a dog-leg hill. There was a thirty metre straight where you could get your speed up, and then you would grab a lamp post, which would catapult you down the hill. I was about halfway down, sitting patiently for the skating sadist to come past. I was ready. I waited and waited and then off he went. He got a great start off and almost didn't make the lamp post— he was going that fast. He catapulted around the dog-leg and was flying. Just before he met the amber assassin— that was me— he was moving like a greyhound. I picked up a house brick and threw it under the wheels as he came passed. The wheels dug into the pavement and he lost control. His legs were everywhere. He kept on going though, picking up speed the whole time, until he came to a sudden halt. An oak tree. He hit it face first and his front teeth and the ones next to them flew in every direction. Perfect.

A friend ran home and told my mom that Seamus had had an accident with a tree. I couldn't possibly run— I was laughing that hard. I could barely breathe.

My mom picked up her handbag, and away she went. She found Seamus in a crumpled mess at the base of the tree, covered in blood and a gaping hole where his teeth used to be. She picked him up, slapped him a few times for shaming her in front of the neighbours, and dragged him home. On the way, she asked me what had happened and, of course, I told her the truth: that Seamus was showing off and lost control on the hill. He was always doing it. M y mom then proceeded to slap him again for being stupid. What a result. It came out better than I thought.

Occasionally, Auntie Helen would come down with her kids, Kevin, Martin and Michael. We would all go to Cannon Hill Park. It was a really nice day out. I liked it when they came down. We had some great laughs together. She had an Austin car. Brand new. In those days it was real leatherette. She was a clever one. IQ of about a hundred and forty-plus. She was a nurse and was a handsome woman. I told her that recently and she said that she still was. She is around seventy now. In later years she was with a fantastic man called Miles Timmons. He passed away recently after a long illness. He as a lovely country man who had time for anyone and everyone. I miss him, and I miss his love for life and his scaffolding. I went to visit him and he was building an extension on his house— one of many. The scaffold he was using was something else. I have never seen anything like it. Tell a lie I have. I was working in Belize, Central America doing charity work, and I saw a scaffold very similar. Miles' scaffold was four metres high and made out of wood. Not the same section wood built with care and precision, but wood that he had obviously found everywhere else but the timber yard. In fields, farms on orange boxes, old fencing and older people wondering why they couldn't stand anymore— because there walking stick was missing. The whole thing was set to collapse, I was sure. We all know that a scaffold is designed to hold man, tools and materials. A sparrow landed on it and the whole thing rocked. He went on it all the same and built the whole extension. Bloody minded Irish. They will do it anyway in spite of you. I will miss him.

Helen was married to a guy called Mick O'Malley back then. Guess what? Another drinker. He used to hit her on a regular basis. She saw sense in the end, but it took her a while. Why does it take such a long time to get out of a toxic relationship? I will never know. Maybe it's because you become infected yourself.

As I said, we would go to Cannon Hill Park, which, to us, was like the country. It was just beautiful. It had a great big duck pond and loads of open space. We used to play football on the grass whilst the others set up the picnic. Life was always good when somebody visited. It was like mom and dad had stuff stashed for the big occasions. Biscuits and cakes when the priest came. Crusty bread and the best butter when relatives came. It was like they were saving the best for everybody else. We did get some occasionally though.

Seamus, of course, always made a fool of himself. He was just crap at football, so we stuck him in goals. Kevin was crap, too, so we stuck him in the other end. Only two on a side, with Martha playing. Mind you she was better than Seamus, so we always had a chance. That is until cock-eyed let the ball in so he could go and pick primroses with Auntie Helen.

Martha was tolerated because of the lady friends that entered our house on a daily basis. She was also tolerated because she would always get different types of jewellery, which would promptly disappear into the Christian McAvoy second-hand sales box. I would wait until all the commotion settled down— of course, denying all knowledge of the articles' whereabouts— and would sell it to a well-known second-hand shop on Coventry Road. I must say that anything that went missing from the house ended up there. I think I was doing a service— recycling. Of course, I didn't do it entirely for the environment. There was also a cash incentive involved. It wasn't much money, but it all went into a little money-box that came in very handy. The money would go mainly towards food. I had this real feeling of hunger all the time. Not just when I was actually hungry. I would think about food continuously— after I had just finished breakfast, coming up to lunch, just after lunch, coming up to dinner, just after dinner. All the bloody time. I think it was because I knew that every time Dad was drinking or depressed, times would be very lean. More often than not, we would only have one meal a day. Although I had a few times when there was nothing. Not often , but a few. We couldn't borrow any money as it was a Tuesday or something, and the milkman, Brian, was on extra watch when he delivered. Those were the days when the money-box would come out. I would then buy the basics— bread, milk, butter and maybe eggs— from a well-known supermarket locally. It was easy shopping there. When I say 'shopping', I actually mean 'acquiring'. My parents knew about it, but I think they turned a blind eye. I was the only one doing it. It was easy. I would always wear baggy clothes, even in summer. I would just take what I needed and one luxury. A packet of biscuits— purely for the taste of something sweet and, of course, the energy. You could last a long time on a packet of biscuits. If I ever got caught it was always at the smaller places. Corner shops and the like. They would only ever clip your ear and throw you out. Never did I get the police taking me away. Oh, apart from one time.

I had been with Francis my cousin, who I would spend time with. Not all the time, but when my mother wasn't falling out with her sister, Theresa. I would just steal out of necessity. Francis would steal for fun.

Theresa and Frank, who was her husband at the time, lived at 1 Slade Road in Sparkhill. They had five children. One day it will come out as the most haunted house in

Birmingham. I swear to this day I have never been so scared as the time I stayed over at their house. The place was so weird. Not a week before, Diana, Francis' sister, had a very restless night, and after waking up for the umpteenth time for no apparent reason, she finally got up and went to the loo. The light was on in the hallway, but not in the toilet, so the room was only lit by the hallway light. Opposite the loo was an old mirror above a wash basin they had found in the cellar. So she just happened to be looking into it from the loo, obviously half asleep. She then said that the mirror lit up just around her face and then the reflection smiled at her. Well, you can imagine the screams. It took hours to console her and she was never the same again. I think she left not long after that.

There was another episode where my mom and I came to the house and we knocked on the door. There was no answer, so my mom opened the letterbox and shouted through. There was no answer. She shouted again, only to then see a small child sitting on the stairs, crying. She shouted to the child, thinking it was Francis. She then told Francis to open the door, and the child replied that he couldn't; he was scared.

"I'm just scared," said the child.

Well, my mom totally confused, then told me to climb through the toilet window at the back of the house. I did this and ran through the house and past the staircase where the child was sat. Francis wasn't there now, but the cellar door was open. I ran as fast as I could and yanked the front door open. She got one step in the door and asked me where Francis was. I said that I hadn't seen him, and she looked through the whole house in every corner and every crevice. No one was to be found. We then made our way downstairs and coming up the garden path was Theresa, Francis and Tony, Francis' older brother. She asked what was going on and we told her the story. Obviously, it wasn't Francis. So who was it? Theresa then told us of a story the previous owners had told her that a young child had fallen down the cellar steps, broken his neck and died. She described the child who she had seen and the clothes he was wearing. That was the same description as the child we talked to. My mom was not happy about this at all, and was visibly shaking. My mom didn't drink much, but Theresa gave her a stiff brandy and settled her down. Seeing one was bad enough, but having a conversation with a ghost was an entirely different matter. We didn't go there much after that, and Mom would never set foot in the place alone.

Theresa always had money and Frank, or 'Maltese Frank', as he was known, was the manager of Stechford swimming baths. We would go there in the summer whenever we could and would get in for free. The pool was fantastic, and it's where they used to have the school swimming competitions. I remember one time Francis and Tony were messing around and tried to see how long they could hold me under the water. I didn't have much choice. They grabbed me and pulled me under the water. I could just about get a foothold at the very end of my breath and pushed myself out of the water. No sooner had I taken a couple of breaths, than I was under again. Once more I managed to get up. Again they dragged me down. I was panicking. I knew that if I didn't get up soon I would drown. I pushed with all my might and started punching at the same time. I caught them both square on the chin and they let go. I continued to punch and was going absolutely crazy. Frank heard the commotion and asked what was going on. I told him they were trying to drown me and I was crying in a rage. He took his belt off and strapped both of them there and then. He never stopped to breathe and they looked like they were wearing stripy pants when they were finished. Only right, too. They didn't do it again.

Where was I? Oh yes, I was with Francis— stealing.

We went to a corner shop on the Stratford road and stole two bottles of Strongbow cider. One each. It was a really hot day and we decided to drink it in the park. I had never drunk before and was only ten. I thought I was Mr. Big, and drank about half the bottle in about ten minutes. I was so ill. The world was spinning way too fast and I couldn't catch up. Francis meanwhile just left me when the park keeper made a move towards us. I couldn't do a thing and welcomed the park keeper's strong arm of support. He sat me in his shed and called the police. He also gave me plenty of water to rehydrate me and by the time the police arrived, I was almost sober again. It was horrendous to feel that way. The police took me to the police station near the city centre and I was booked. The shop keeper pressed charges and I had to appear in court. They slapped me on the wrist and told me not to be stupid again. That was my one and only appearance in court. I have never been charged with anything again.

2

Lead or Copper, Not Zinc

I'M NOT SAYING I DIDN'T LEARN MY LESSON. The scrape with the law taught me a lot. I definitely had respect for the law, and I made sure I didn't get caught again. I continued to steal. I had to. I never stole off people, like burglaries or cars or muggings. Nothing personal. I just stole to provide for the lean days. Like tatting.

For those of you who are not familiar with the word 'tatting', I shall explain. It is the collection of metal to sell in the scrap yard. I would take all kinds of metals. Back then, as now, copper sold at the best price and it was impossible to get a good wage from that. It is so light you would have to fill a truck to get a good price. A truck I couldn't drive. A bus, maybe— if I had been quicker— but a truck, no. So I stuck to lead. That was a good thing for me.

I would 'case the joint' first and would know exactly where to go and where to hide the loot after. I would take my go-cart and some tools from my dad's toolbox. I had a little toolbox of my own on the back of the cart made from wood, and it had a door and a lock— perfect for all the tools I would need. And, just in case I had to repair the cart, I also had bits and bobs and some oil. I loaded the cart with the tools I thought I might need: cutters, a hacksaw, a small crow bar and screwdrivers of different sizes.

The job was normally flashings around low level roofs. I would climb up the drainpipe late at night and start to prise away at the flashings. I would then roll it up as small as possible and drop it into a secluded spot from the roof. I would do the whole job then climb down. If the drainpipe was made of lead, that would go as well. If it was made of zinc, it would stay. You could tell by the weight— lead is much heavier.

I would then load up my go-cart and head towards home. At the back of our house was a bomb peck. A bit of waste ground where a house had been earlier, before it was bulldozed. It looked a little bit like the old war pictures where the houses had been hit and only rubble left— hence 'bomb peck'. Next to this was a railway line that ran right next to my back garden. I would go on to the embankment of the railway track and stash all my lead and bits of copper, or whatever I had, and before it got too much to hide and, of course, carry, I weighed it in. The most I ever got in one load was twenty-two pounds. A week's wages for a labourer in 1974 was about nineteen pounds. I was absolutely delighted. I spoke to the man there who I got to know very well and told him the story of what was going on. He said that whatever I had, he would take. He knew it was illegal, but he also knew that it was a case of survival. Just doing what you had to, to get by. That was all. The money went straight into the money-box and it was a good time for a while. Until it ran out and it was time to start again. There were other schemes, too.

There was a sweet warehouse not far from where we lived. Imagine that: a sweet *warehouse*. I didn't even know about it until the school, in its wisdom, decided to have a school trip there. What a brilliant idea. Whoever thought of that deserved a very big prize. I think it was Mr. Scott. A genius.

It was probably about a kilometre or so from my place, and it was quite secluded on an industrial estate, right next door to a Walkers Crisps warehouse. Bloody Heaven.

Well, well, well. What can I tell you about that place? A lot, actually. As soon as we stepped in the door, I could tell you where the weak spots were. There was a very old man who was the warehouse assistant, a labourer who just swept up and kept the place clean— who worked only on Saturday mornings— and a secretary. That was it. On Sundays, they were closed.

So, from Saturday afternoon until Monday morning the place was empty. No alarms back then, so I hatched a plan.

I would gather an array of tools from the trusty old toolbox and I would break in. I also bought a set of tin snips from *the* second hand shop on Coventry Road. Well, not exactly bought— more 'acquired'. Once I had what I thought I might need, it was on. I went back to the factory on Saturday morning and spoke to the sweeper upper and, with pad in hand, told him that I needed more questions answered for my school project. Being the important man he was for that split second, he was only too pleased to help. I asked him questions like 'how are the sweets stored and how often are they moved around?' and 'there were sweets stacked five or six pallets high. What happens to the ones on the bottom?'. The questions kept coming, and the chief sweeper upper played along. Not realising, of course, that he was being conned by a master criminal. Well, I thought I was, anyway. After about an hour or so I left fully conversed in the ways and workings of the sweet industry.

Now for the second part of the plan. I went to the local newsagents and fluttered my big cow eyes at the lady behind the counter and asked for a quarter of humbugs. She was a bit blind and a bit deaf. Nothing going for her really, but I could tell she loved me. You just do, don't you?

Anyway, she gave me my humbugs and I gave her twenty pence. Before I could turn away with my sweeties, she gave me change back for twenty pence. I would normally turn and run, but today was different. I told her she had made a mistake and that I had only given her ten pence, and I returned my ten pence back to her. Smart or what?

She was over the moon. She came around from the other side of the counter and started saying, with this high pitched voice, "Well, what an honest young man you are. Do you hear that, Maude? What did I tell you? I could see it in his eyes. And just look at those curls. As honest as the day is long. Good lad. Here, have the sweets for nothing— you have just made my day, love." and gave me back my ten pence.

With my halo slipping and my wings snagging on the light fittings, I proceeded to tell my story of my school project. I also told her that it was my job to collect fifty paper bags— just small ones big enough for a quarter of sweets, for my part in the project. I would, of course, be happy to pay for them.

"Not at all," she said. She gave me the bags and a few sweets more, and gave me a hug on the way out. "And if you need any more, come and see me."

I was brilliant. Eight years old and I would easily have won an award if someone had seen it. Anyone, in fact. I did feel a bit bad about the way I had duped her. However, she was happy to give the bags after I had returned the money, so one good turn deserves another, as they say in the driving schools.

The third part of the plan was the most difficult: breaking into the sweet warehouse. It was planned for a Saturday night when my dad was working. I stashed the tools earlier in the day behind the warehouse in some bushes, and the plan was ready to go. Even if my dad had been working one week and had nine off previously, on the Saturday, he would go out. No saving here; Dad needs a pint. As I said, he had had a hard week that week and he thought he deserved a pint. He was too tired on the Friday and had his usual beer and sleeping tablets at home, so he was well rested for partying. The ex-servicemen's club was the place he would frequently go to— with or without the family. We all went, and, of course, Seamus was in his stripy jumper and Oxford bags. Martha had something she had just thrown on, apparently. That's what she told her friends, anyway. When in reality it had taken the best part of eighteen hours to get it right. I wore black. Black side pockets, black polo neck and black plimsolls— ninety-nine pence from Woolworths. As if I actually bought them. I was set.

The night took its usual course. There was a band, then a little bit later a disco. There was lots of beer, lots of cigarettes. Passive smoking? We were professionals at passive smoking then. I could have been an Olympic champion. I could have been someone.

The clock seemed to go in slow motion. I was waiting for 9 p.m. to strike. That's when the Bingo would start and I normally disappeared then anyway. I would go and play snooker or darts with my pals. However, not that night. I had other plans. Finally, 9 p.m. arrived, and I was gone— straight onto my go-cart and down to the warehouse. I looked around. The night was quite warm and all I could hear was my heart thumping— nothing like a bit of adrenalin to kick start something naughty. There was a hazy orange light on the front of the building, but nothing on the back. It was the end of summer, so it was still quite light, but was getting darker by the minute. I waited about ten minutes— although it seemed like an hour— just sat on my go-cart in the dark, waiting for the right time to start.

Finally, I started working on the metal sheeting on the

outside the warehouse. With my newly bought, uh-um, I mean, 'acquired', tin snips. I made light work of the tin, even for an eight-year-old. It was easy going up the sheet, but across was a bit harder. The profile was quite heavy and I took longer to go across than I had imagined. I had made an L-section cut just big enough for me to slide inside when I needed to. Between the sheets there was a heavy insulation, so I knifed a square section out and dropped it to the floor. There was, however, a second layer, but instead of cutting this with the snips, the metal was so old I just prized the sheet free from its mountings. I was in. I slid down inside the panel and was directly behind the rows of pallets I had seen in my project research earlier. I got my bicycle lamp out and turned it on quietly. The pallet in front of me lit up. I shone it up to the roof and down the line to the far end of the row. On every pallet was not just one variety of sweets, but every variety you could think of.

Chocolate limes, humbugs, chocolate raisins, boiled sweets, all different colours jelly beans, black jacks, fruit salads. There were also my favourite: sweet peanuts, sherbet lemons and Coltsfoot rock. They had them all. They were packed in big glass jars. The kind of jars you get in sweet shops on the back shelf. The kind of jars you wished you had, just once in your life. I balanced the light on my lap and cut the protective wrapping. I pulled at one of the jars— a jar of chocolate limes— and it slipped into my lap, knocking over the light. I picked up the jar and turned off the lamp. When my eyes adjusted to the light, I pushed the jar through the panel onto the ground outside with my lamp. I then pushed myself through, put the insulation back in and wedged the external panel back into place. My heart was beating wildly and I just sat there in the dark, trying to calm down a little and just to make sure that no one was around when I made my exit. The bushes covered me nicely and I took my time to make sure it was clear. I then loaded my go-cart and scarpered.

I don't think I ever went so fast. Thankfully, everything went in the little toolbox at the back of my go-cart, including the sweets, and I slipped the padlock back into place. I pulled up outside the ex-servicemen's club at 9:58 p.m. I ran to the toilet, brushed myself down, and washed my hands and face. I then walked in as calm as you like and sat down at our table. My mom asked me where I had been, and I said I had been playing snooker in the games room. She told me not to spend so much time in there as it was full of drunks. I told her I wouldn't and that was that. I then said maybe it was time I went home on my cart, because it was getting late. She asked me if I had brought the lamp with me so I could see on the pavement and I said I had. She gave me the key and away I went. I took my stash home and hid it at the back of my wardrobe underneath all my old games. Over the next two weeks I sold the whole jar at school and to my friends in the grove. I made nine pounds and a few fillings. I went back to the warehouse five times more and even took orders. They were happy days. The thing is to know when a good thing has to stop. I went back one day and the panel had been repaired and a light fitted on the back. The scam was over, but it was good while it lasted.

3

Pleasant Park— Home Sweet Home

WE LIVED IN A MAISONETTE. SOUNDS QUAINT, DOESN'T IT? It wasn't. Almost Parisian? It wasn't. It wasn't anything like quaint or Parisian. It was a concrete three-bedroom flat with one coal fire in the living room and steel-framed, single-glazed windows. In summer, it was like an oven, and the winters were a living Hell. It was a fight for the coats most evenings. I think, apart from the psychological problems I had, which were missed by the authorities and everyone around me— but I'm not bitter— this was the reason why I wet the bed. Until I was thirty-six. Not really; it was until I was thirteen. It was freezing cold and, except for that brief respite of warm urine in my pyjamas, I almost froze to death most evenings. Seamus used to get up in the middle of the night, and take the coats off me, and so I would wake up shivering in a pool of cold urine. Bedsores were visible and it looked like I had nappy rash all the time. Try explaining that to your football team mates.

The whole flat was overrun with mice and many times I woke up with a mouse running across my face. I once woke up— wet again— with a dead mouse in the hole where I had continually wet the bed and the mattress had collapsed. It had drowned!

There was linoleum everywhere, and not much luxury. 'Shiny carpet', my dad called it.

"It's actually better than carpet, son, because, if you spill your drinks on it, you can sponge it right up."

I was impressed.

There was one luxury, actually.

The water heater had a blanket around it that didn't itch. I think it was happy. I'm sure I saw it smile once.

We, on the other hand, had blankets made from the wool from a sheep's bum and barbed wire; stitched together with Brillo pad. They were old army issue, given to us by the army welfare, which looked after dad and us for many years after he left the army.

My parents shared the biggest bedroom just off the living room. I remember once I was sent to their bedroom for being naughty and the council had fitted a new gas fire. I was really mad at being sent to bed early for something I had obviously done, but didn't want to be punished for. I was bored. Bored. Bored. Bored. Bored. Bored. The word bored even sounds boring, doesn't it? Anyway, the gas fire was interesting, though, so I turned it on, as I was really cold in mid July— high eighties. Well you would be, wouldn't you? The fire burst into life and the glow was fascinating. I found some paper and pushed it through the grill. The flame traced up the paper and I held it high so the flame burnt down slowly then down to make it quicker. Then high to make it slower again. I blew it out just before it reached my fingers.

That was fun, I thought. *I will do that again.*

So I did. Same scenario, only this time halfway through the burning, I heard someone coming. I didn't have a chance to blow it out, so I just threw it under the bed.

My mom entered and asked if I was asleep. I said I was and she left the room in a huff for me being so smart. After a few minutes I thought something might be wrong as smoke began to appear at the top of the ceiling. I wondered where it came from and then realised that the paper under the bed might not have gone out like it was supposed to. Bloody unreliable paper. You could never rely on paper burning out when it was supposed to.

I ran to the door and told my parents that the bed was on fire.

"Don't be stupid!" they cried. "And get back to bed."

I went back in the room. A few minutes later, I went out again. "Mom! The bed really is on fire!"

"Look, I'm not telling you again. Get back to bed. If I have to get up, there will be trouble," she said in a very frustrated tone.

I went back in the room for the second and final time. The bed was really going now. Fire danced across the bed sheets and was making its way up the velour headboard. The smoke was thick and was creeping its way down the walls.

I'm going to die, I thought. *This is it. Death by toasting. No, I can't die like this.*

"Mom!" I shouted. "The bed really, really is on fire!"

This time, she saw the smoke billowing out of the door and jumped. For a big lady she could hit some kilometres per hour. Fantastic. Supermom, cook, cleaner and now fire fighter. Quicker than quick she was in the bedroom and dousing the flames. Dad was a little slower, but joined the action as fast as his slippers would carry him— after watching the ending to the Morcambe and Wise summer special, of course. Cool, my dad.

They used all kinds of things to put the fire out: old tea that was sitting on the bedside table, water in glasses, something else in a glass— I didn't know what it was, and didn't ask— clothes, petrol, I think— everything. After some time, the fire was out. The heroes of the day had done a sterling job with no loss of life. Bravo, bravo. I told them that they were brilliant. I did actually tell them that.

For some reason, they began asking awkward questions like: 'how did that happen? What were you doing? Are you trying to kill us all? Why can you never do what you are told?'.

The usual answers were given: 'I don't know. It wasn't me. I didn't do it; it just started burning. I did have curry for tea, and you know how that can be'. *Smack*.

To this day, it remains the story of how the bed spontaneously combusted. That was my story anyway, until now. Oh crap.

I shared a bedroom with Seamus, the middle room, and Martha had a room for herself. Because she was a girl. I do not know how many times I heard that growing up. No, but she's a girl. She's a girl. She's a girl. I know she's a girl, but what does that have to do with welding?

Her bedroom was opposite the bathroom at the end of the landing. The bathroom had the usual fittings. Toilet tissue was a luxury we could ill afford, so we had to use newspaper. Handy enough whilst on the loo. You could not only use the paper for wiping your bum at the end of a number two, you could also read what was happening on the stock exchange in New York. Which is what every eight-year-old inner city kid was interested in, weren't they? The bath was used only on a Sunday, whether it was needed or not. First, my mom ,then dad would go in. Then we would let a bit of water out and warm it up a bit. Then it was my sister, Martha. Then the same thing. Cold water out, hot water in. Then Seamus. Of course, him being who he was, the process would be a bit different. He went in. Colder water out, hot water in. Even more water in until all the hot water had run out. He would then soak and soak until the water went cold. He would then take in his bike and clean that until the water was absolutely black. He would then shout for me and tell me that the bath was ready for me. I didn't bathe much. I just sat in the sink and swilled the bits that didn't see much daylight. I would then wash the bits that saw a lot of daylight and left the mud in the bath to itself. I then went to the airing cupboard in the hallway that housed the water heater. Thrown over the heater were the towels. Of course, Seamus had taken the remaining two and would be flossing his loins with my towel. What a brother he is. One day. One day.

There, with the basics, was a small kitchen. It did, however, have a fantastic gas stove. There is nothing like toast on a gas stove. It is a special taste and one I will never forget. The kitchen overlooked a balcony. My father fell off this when he was drunk when I was about eleven, and broke his shoulder and collar bone. He said he heard burglars. He said he wasn't drunk, but was holding his pint glass until he hit the ground. Never spilt a drop. Brown ale.

Dad (on the left) with a pal during a session. Handsome, isn't he? Hollywood...

The curse of many a housewife back then. Burglars would have been absolutely hammered by the women of the community back then, never mind the men. We lived in a small cul de sac. Again, that French feel, yet really it was a grove with about twenty families. Mainly Irish. A few Jamaican families, who, I'm afraid to say, had a torrid time, and one Indian family. The Jamaican families were exotic, to say the least. I think that's where my fondness for foreign food came from. Christopher was a member of one Jamaican family who lived on the ground floor in the same block as the Maloneys. He was a great marbles player. He was a great lad. A great artist, too. He was tall and wiry and had an infectious laugh. I really liked him. What a sweet left foot and, I have to say, he could take a good punch and deliver just as well. He was wiry, but as strong as an ox. I met him a few times later when we were older, and he was still exactly the same. A very, very nice guy. He was a good friend to a school pal of mine, Davinder Singh. Another great geezer. I used to go around to his house a lot during my school days. After my brother's near-death experience, I embraced other cultures wholeheartedly. I was like a ginger, afro-headed George Harrison. I even started playing the sitar and called everybody 'man'.

I heard in later years that Christopher died in a car accident. When I was told, I kept thinking of this no-nonsense kid who would do anything for you; a kind and gentle soul who never stopped laughing. It's strange, but we lost contact— apart from the odd occasion when bumping into him— when I moved from Pleasant park when I was thirteen. However, at that moment in time, I missed him. I hadn't seen him in ten years or more, but I was sad.

The parents in the grove kept themselves to themselves and didn't really argue. Surprising really, but considering the amount of kids and the amount of potential trouble, it was actually relatively quiet. Maybe it was because when you did see it erupt externally and was surrounded by violence within the home, it was normal.

The grove was a close-knit little community. The kind

of community that, when trouble erupted, would be baying for blood, but would also back every member up outside the grove. In the street we were one big family. In the grove we were just dogs with other dogs. You had to look after yourself. I was fighting everyday— it's just the way it was. There was a pecking order and if it wasn't followed you would be smacked back into line. There was, as I said, about twenty families with about twenty kids. It was a constant battle from the time you got up to the time you went to bed. If it wasn't the kids who tried it on, it was the parents knocking hell out of you. I remember my mom once hit me with a frying pan whilst she was cooking eggs. Never spilt a drop of lard, and the eggs remained in the pan. Perfection. The timing was impeccable. I didn't actually realise what hit me until the old grease was thick in my afro and making its way down my face. She wasn't a violent woman. I suppose she was just frustrated about the fact that she had told me twenty times not to do something, and then just snapped. I can still hear the ringing. That's probably why I am a bit special today. Not special in a nice way, but special in a mentally ill way. However, it could never be proved. No certificate or anything. I still have the dent on the side of my head. She did, however, hit Seamus often with a stick. Not enough for my liking. She once threw a shoe at Seamus and it went through the landing door window. Of course, Seamus got the blame for that and got cracked again. Oh, happy days.

As I said though, violence was normal. You just lived with it. You do not realise something is very wrong until you compare it with something else. You then think that there is another world, which, unfortunately, some people never know. I was lucky— or just plain intuitive— to distinguish between the two, and craved for better things. Teachers in school became the role models and the kinds of people I would love to become. I was already searching for something better, even at the age of seven or eight, and realised that I would not remain in the circle into which I had been born. I tried to escape when I was about three or four on my bike down the concrete steps. I went from top to bottom and was just about to go through the glazed door when my dad walked in and caught me. Damn it, almost there.

It wasn't that I was any better than anyone else. I just knew there was more to life than drink, violence and abuse. I didn't understand that my dad was sick— I just thought that everybody's dad was the same. My childhood was a mixture of three or four different lives. One at home, one at school, one where I looked at the everyday survival, and one where I shut myself out of the abuse at the hands of people who thought it was normal, but with a twist. What is normal anyway? What is normal for one is certainly not normal for another. I did not know what normal was.

4
Families

THE MALONEYS: THOMAS, TERRY, ROBBIE AND CAROL. The O'Haras: Christopher, Veronica, Peter, George and Jane, I think. The Smiths: Mark, Peter, Patrick and Jane. The McAvoys: that's us.

These were the main families and the others had one or two children.

The Maloneys

THE MALONEYS WERE A TOUGH LOT. THE MOTHER, Kathleen, was a real handsome woman. She took nothing from no one— a no-nonsense woman. Her husband, Tommy, was a lovely fella. He was a small, wiry little man, but also a no-nonsense type. You had to be in control in those days or your kids would take over. The parents were respected, regardless of how they behaved themselves. Whether it was by fear or by love, they were respected. Thomas, the eldest child, was also a good looking lad and had his fare share of ladies. One I remember was called Gill, and what a cracker she was. Lovely nature, too. Thomas, however, had a temper and he was most definitely the toughest lad in the grove. He could take on anybody. He

27

would take no prisoners when it came to the kids or his two younger brothers, Terry and Robbie. They would get it just as much as anyone else.

Terry was about four years older than me. Also a good looking lad, but a bit heavy. Not fat, mind you, just heavy-set. He liked to throw his weight around, too. I remember more than once I would argue with him and I would probably land one or two. Then he took over and that would be the end of it. I remember one particular argument where he took my scooter and threw it onto the road. I got really mad and just belted him. It did nothing but get him mad, and he hit me so many times that I thought I was surrounded. He was a boxer, you see, and I was just a street fighter. He had movement, style and left-right, hook, cross followed with the big right hand. I was covered in blood and wondering what the hell I had got myself into. I wondered was it too late to say sorry for soiling his knuckles on my face. Or should I just get out of there and run. No, running was for girls and I was no girl. I hit him again. This made him even angrier and he sat on my arms as I was flat on my back. Now my face was pointing towards the sky and his fists were coming in relatively quickly. Quick enough to realise that I was a goner. What they refer to in the trade as 'dead'. He pummelled me until he thought I had enough, which wasn't my plan, I can tell you. He then got up. I got up, too, and, in my wisdom, asked, "Is that the best you can do?"

He pummelled me again. He got up again. I got up again. I didn't say anything. We both walked home.

The O'Haras

BIG CHRIS O'HARA, THE HEAD OF THE FAMILY, WAS a great bloke when sober, and a terrible singer when not. He was a big football fan, and loved Everton football club. I'm not sure if he came from Liverpool, but the passion he had for the blues was second to none.

"Everton... Everton..."

It was a popular song most Friday nights with Chris. Late at night or early morning, after one too many, he would aspire to the great heights of the song and dance man, and perform to his heart's content to a crowd peering through curtains and shushing their kids back to bed.

This was all normal stuff in the grove. I think his favourite player was Bob Latchford. He was one of the greatest players of his day. Strong, could run against the defenders, and rose like a salmon in the air. Brilliant!

Young Christopher O'Hara was a tall, good looking lad. He had the pick of most girls and had the gift of the gab to go with it. He was my hero. He was a real ladies' man. I loved his sister, too— Veronica. A dark-haired beauty five years older than me, but that didn't matter. Not to me, anyway. I never had a chance. I was a red-headed, freckle-faced, piss-the-bed and smelled most days apart from Sunday. The problem was Veronica saw me most days, smelled me most days. She was best friends with Martha, my sister, and would often come around and listen to David Cassidy or the Osmonds. There was, of course, the tartan brigade; the Bay City Rollers. They were all great hitters of the day. She used to play the records on an old record player at full blast knowing full well she could do what she wanted when she had friends around.

Whenever Veronica came around, I used to make every excuse to suck up to her. Cups of tea, toast, etcetera. Whatever there was in the cupboards— which wasn't much— she could have. I made a special effort to make sure she was comfortable. I would run errands, drop letters off to boys she fancied, or go to the shop, clean the records between plays, and stack them ready to go. Martha had another good friend, too: Mary McAde. She was just gorgeous. I followed her around like a lapdog. Nine years old and I was in love with about ten girls. All out of my league, because Chris O'Hara said that, if you aim for as many girls as you can out of your league, the law of averages states that you must get one. I didn't get any.

Mary was at the top of the list. She was also Irish Catholic and stunning. I remember she stayed over sometimes. One night, I snuck into my sister's room when they were asleep. Mary was facing me. I bent down, trembling like mad, and planted a smacker straight on her lips. I stayed there for what seemed like a very, very, long time— it was probably a microsecond— and then released my grip. It was wonderful. In the previous meetings I had looked at her, smelled her perfume and sat on her lap. She knew damn well I had a crush on her as big as a Yorkie bar, and played on it. She would tease me a bit and make me blush, but I didn't mind. Just to be in her company was everything to me.

Now I had kissed her. Me, pissy, smelly Christian McAvoy, had kissed Mary McAde. Okay, she didn't know about it, but it still counted. I still count it to this day. I kissed her, so there.

Kevin O'Hara was the same age as me, and we competed in most things. He had a great sense of humour and was what the doctors called a 'pyromaniac'. I wasn't quite sure about the 'pyro' part, but 'maniac' was about right. Set fire to everything he could. He loved it. The glow of the flame made his face light up in more ways than one. A really good lad— a great lad, in fact. The only thing was that a box of matches meant more to him than life itself. We fought together, laughed together and ran away together when we heard the fire engines sirens.

Peter was a little smaller than us, but a great goalkeeper. He really got stuck in, too. Marbles came next and he had the hand-eye coordination of a champion archer. Unbelievable.

The Smiths

MARK WAS A STOCKY LAD— TALL AND STRONG LIKE AN OX. He proved that more than once when he knocked the crap out of me. It's not surprising, really. I stood my ground a lot and didn't think too much about the fact that I would probably get hammered if I didn't keep my mouth shut. I got punched a lot. Maybe it was because Mark was big that I thought I might see how far I could push him. I would definitely say that he was a patient lad. A very patient lad. I drove him insane. I remember very clearly that he was crying one day and that surprised me. I asked him what was wrong and he said that his grandmother had just died. Now, I know now, and knew then, that he was fond of his grandmother. So why, in my wisdom, did I say she was a silly old cow anyway and it was time she went?

Mark had recently broken his left arm in an accident and his arm was covered in plaster of Paris, all the way from the wrist to the shoulder. I thought this was my chance, whilst he is injured, to get him mad, and then I could take him. Smash his face in, the snotty git.

He stood, belted me about six times with the plaster cast, and pushed me off a high wall, which led down to some waste ground. Not once, but twice. Why did I keep going back? I was never going to win this one. Just call it a day and keep your ginger mouth shut.

No, no. I just kept going at him. Stupid. It wasn't the first time and it wasn't the last.

I did help him though— a few weeks later. Opposite our house was a row of derelict terraced houses. They were due for demolition and the kids had stripped them of anything valuable and anything that wasn't, for that matter. Between the outhouse and the back door of these derelict houses was a washing area, and the kids had broken every pane of glass and every bottle they could get their hands on, in this area. Mark was jumping from one outhouse to another and he slipped. He landed on approximately twenty broken bottles and was a complete mess. I pulled him out. He just ambled on home and told his mom what had happened. He was rushed to hospital and I think he had over two hundred stitches to one side of his body. He wasn't much different to a road map for a while. Madness.

Inside the terraced houses was a playground for the kids. We used to climb on the roofs and slide between the valleys, and climb down the drainpipe playing *Follow my leader*. Absolutely deadly. Mark was the leader most of the time as he was the oldest. And if anyone got into trouble, he would be the one to pull us out of it. He was an athlete as well as strong. A complete all-rounder.

Peter was the same age as me and, like his brother Mark, had trouble with keeping colds and flues within the confines of his nose. It was like two candles permanently attached to his top lip. By wax, probably.

Patrick was an epileptic. It was horrendous. Whenever he got excited he would go down and go into this terrifying fit. We all used to hold him down and he would go blue. That was the sequence of events about four times a day. His mom or Mark would then take him home. Jesus, what a life.

Mark's mom, Doreen, was a frail, skinny woman with a heart of gold. She would walk really quickly, even when fully laden with shopping and kids. She took care of the house whilst her husband, Frank, went to work as a dustman. He was a big strapping man of around 1.97 metres tall, and weighed around 130 kilos. Never forget that the bins in those days were steel, not plastic like today, and

Frank used to toss them on his back like bags of crisps. He was like a man mountain to us kids in those days. A huge, humble man. A gentleman, as I recall.

5

To Fight or Not to Fight— That is the Question

MICHAEL WAS ANOTHER JAMAICAN KID IN THE GROVE. He lived next door to Christopher in another block. A short, stocky lad— just like his father. They were a religious family and every Sunday they would go to church. A Methodist or Pentecostal church, I believe. They would be dressed in their Sunday bests and I must say they looked really smart. I don't think I have ever seen shirts so white. They were so bright they dazzled in the sun and blinded you. Michael was a kind, peaceful kid, but his dad was really strict. I saw him smack Michael a few times and the door close behind him, and then the screams as he climbed the stairs. No shortage of violence there. I think he had a bloody nose or cut or something every day. Something that the other lads had done to him. I myself threw a brick at him and split his head open. I don't know why I did it. Arguing over marbles, probably. Lost my rag and the next thing I was in my flat waiting for my world to boil over. I heard his dad coming from three hundred metres away, followed by a bludgeoning on the door with his great fists as he demanded retribution. The man was screaming at the top of his lungs for about five minutes, demanding that I be flogged with a stick until the blood flows.

34

Normally when fathers are face to face it turns into a right battle. Everybody knew it.

There was a real crowd. Loads of kids hanging off fences, pretending not to be there. Women and children, babes in arms. Drunks and dads. Dads who were drunk. Mothers with their washing on their arms. Mothers with kids on their arms.

People were taking bets, money had passed hands and there were odds forecasts. The fight was on.

People were waiting with baited breath. Hardly breathing. Waiting for the first punch and then it was game on.

My dad told him as calm as a nun that he would deal with it and turned and walked away, pushing me in front. The man was so stunned that he himself became calm, turned on his heels and went home— he, too, pushing his offspring ahead. Trying to stem the blood with his immaculate white shirt.

Nothing. Nothing at all. People were saying things like 'bloody hell, is that it? All bets off'.

People turned away as if in disgust. Crap. Boo. Kids went home. Women folded there washing, and then let the kids down. Dads kept on drinking, complaining of the poor entertainment, and then went home. They all knew that my dad could handle himself and was quick as lightning with the head butt. It could have all been over in seconds and the crowd would have gone home, proud that a fellow Irishman had yet again proved how tough he was.

No one could understand it. Why didn't he just do what he normally does?

I couldn't understand it. This is what people do around here. They settle differences with a bloody good punch-up. No calling the police or any rubbish like that. You settled it man to man. Draw the line and it's one punch for him and one punch for you.

It wasn't as though I wanted my dad to fight. It was just expected. I loved my dad and certainly didn't want him to get hurt. It was just that there were laws in our little world that had to be adhered to, or you were shunned. Or worse, you were shunned for something your brother or your sister did. But to be shunned for something my dad had done... That surprised me.

I was a bit disappointed and a bit ashamed. I thought my dad was just going to belt him and tell him to piss off. He didn't. I thought that Michael's dad was going to belt my dad. He didn't. I didn't understand. What just happened here?

My dad took me upstairs and gave me a right good hiding. He actually told me why he didn't do anything. He said that you have to pick your fights. You don't pick fights against other dads over their kids fighting. That doesn't happen, because in five minutes they will be friends again. No point fighting over that. However, what I had done, I would pay for. He did not give me a hiding often, but that day I deserved it. I accepted it. I did deserve it. I knew it then and I know it now. The next day Michael and I were best friends again and playing marbles as usual, just like nothing had happened. My dad was right!

6

Up, Up and Away, and King to Knight Five

YEP, DAD WAS A DRINKER AND HAD A DEPENDENCY on sleeping pills. What is the point of escapism when all you do is fall asleep? If you didn't get it— that was a joke.

I think, according to the symptoms of that bygone age, Dad was bi-polar. When he was up, he was flying. He would go to work, earn a bit of cash, and put food in the cupboards. There was coal in the fire, and money for the electricity meter and the television meter. It was a black and white television. Try watching snooker on a black and white television. The balls are all different shades of grey. Complete guesswork until the balls collided and the commentator told you what he was going for or just hit. I lost count at the amount of times the telly ran out when there was a film on. Every time it came to the exciting bit, it would just cut out. Dad, however, had his stack of linoleum fifty pence pieces, so the matinee could resume. We used the same method for the electricity meter, too. It worked a treat. I never really thought of the consequences. You just did what you had to. I remember the TV man came to empty the meter a few times. I think the rent was about four pounds a week. I don't remember much money ever going into the slot, so I didn't know why he came at all.

Anyway, he took whatever he could get and gave Dad back
the lino money. He said he didn't have much use for it
locally and, obviously, my dad had found a use for it, so
why take it? When Dad wasn't working, we hid from
everybody.

When Dad had his good times, we had normal food and
even apple pies after the bath on Sundays. We would sit
down to *Little house on the Prairie* and go to bed early for
school the next day. I liked those Sundays, and never
wanted them to end.

A full belly, with real lemonade in your glass. Happy
days. However, they were numbered. You knew they
wouldn't last. We just lived the days as they unfolded, and,
when darkness crept over my dad over a period of time,
you knew it was time to pull the belt in. It wasn't only the
fact that the sickness kept him off work. There was
national depression to think of, too. There were lots of
unemployed people and when you were only able to work
in short periods, it was hopeless. There were fewer jobs
available to a man like my dad, so, when he couldn't find
work when he was up, he became depressed because of
that. It was a constant battle. It was a constant battle for us
all.

He was a fantastic bloke when he was up, but, when he
came down... My mom knew it, too. Nothing ever lasted
long, it seemed. He got more irritated with everybody.

Morcombe and Wise were no longer funny and even
Frank Spencer couldn't make him laugh— not even on his
roller skates. He would drink more and eat less. That
wasn't hard, though, because in this stage he didn't have
work - Didn't want it. Couldn't find it. There wasn't any.
Not the right job. Not the right pay. Too far away. Too
close.

Mom used to get out her walking shoes, and we'd go
asking friends, relatives, non-relatives and non-friends for a

few bob. Just for a loaf of bread and some milk for the kids. If she had some left, for the bingo. I don't know how many times I passed a note to somebody with the words written in pencil: 'Can you lend us a few bob until Friday? Nellie'.

God Almighty, if it wasn't for my mom, we would have starved to death completely. Bingo, to be honest, was the only thing she did. Oh, and darts. She loved darts, and was bloody good, too.

On bingo nights, which were most nights— sometimes the early session, sometimes the late— she would go through the same routine. She would set Dad up with a couple of bottles of brown ale, and my younger brother and I would be watching the telly.

"Any trouble, come and get me. Wish me luck. Ta-ra!" Then she was gone.

My dad had a habit then of wanting to play chess. I learnt very early that he would never finish the game. Seamus was out and Martha was with her pals or boyfriends. They would both be in late, so it was just me and my little brother in. Knowing full well that he would be out for the count when she got back. Cigarette burning away in his fingers— that I would have to take out and put out. Then settle his drink on the table and put a blanket over him so he didn't freeze.

He would also take a few sleeping tablets when we weren't looking, so I was always amazed at how strong this drink was. I had no idea he was mixing the two. In two hours he would be on his way, slurring his words. Then he passed out. I would wrap him up, and Mom would put him to bed when she came in.

She knew there wouldn't be any trouble. What trouble could a sleeping man make?

We would stay up until Mom came home, just in case he tried to go to the toilet or something.

It was a nightmare. I was eight years old and looking

after my little brother, who was three at the time, when I can first remember what was going on. I couldn't understand why Dad had a big medicine hunt when Mom left the flat. He was addicted and just couldn't do without them. So we used to have the tablet hunt and think it was just a game. When we found them, Dad would be delighted and pat us on the head and laugh a bit. Of course, when she came home, it would all go crazy again. In the morning, he never remembered anything, and Mom would sulk for a bit. Dad would just tell her to shut up. He would then tell her to go and get some more drink. Even if she had no money, she would have to bring drink home or Dad would just throw her out again. That sickness was driving us all crazy. How frustrating it must have been for her. Of course, she just lived for the good days and survived the bad days, like every good Irish Catholic wife should do. I'm sure she wasn't alone then and not alone now.

I couldn't blame her at the time for going to the bingo—it was her release. It was her time. Not much for a woman who put up with that shit two weeks in the month.

When Dad was working, it wasn't all plain sailing, either. Many a time, I would go with Mom on a Friday and stand outside the factory gates— or wherever he was working— and wait for Dad to come out. She would then ask for the rent, food and the bills money before he went off to the pub with his pals and drink the lot. I remember he used to tell her to piss off and tell her not to embarrass him in front of his mates. She stood her ground though and got some money eventually. He said he would only be an hour and not return until the pubs had closed— penniless and sometimes even owing money to one or two. It was hopeless, really. Why she never left, I have no idea. Although, with four kids it would have been tough and, anyway, she still loved him. We all did.

That's when my little schemes came in handy. My

mom would often ask me if I had money, and most of the time I said no, knowing full well that half would be spent on drink, cigarettes and a little bit on basics, milk, bread and butter.

All the bills were mainly paid at the end of the week. Friday at teatime. In those days, you got a wage packet with the money in, and, if you came after Friday, most would be gone and you wouldn't get paid. They would knock a special knock and you knew who it was by that.

It didn't really matter who came to the door— they hardly ever got paid. We were always in arrears with everything. When the new milkman, Brian, started, my mom got everything from him to begin with and, of course, paid what she could. When she won the bingo at Pontin's, she paid a lot off the bill. Dad didn't want her to, but she did anyway. She was always in the doghouse for something.

Brian, on the other hand, was an angel. He was also an Irishman and he lived with his red-haired wife, who had just moved over from Ireland. Of course, he had seen it all before. However, he was a real gentleman and, every time she said she couldn't pay, he told her that if she just paid a couple of quid off the bill, it would keep the bosses off his back.

I think that, when she didn't pay anything, he put some money in himself. He knew we were in trouble, and just kept helping us. He truly had a heart of gold. I don't know how many times I took milk off the cart when he wasn't looking or when he was talking to my mom. But you had to be quick. We lived above Mr. and Mrs. Williams, and they had three children— Susan, Diane and David. The girls were gorgeous, but David was a loner. He never mixed with the poor lot. His family were quite well-to-do and had a bit of money. It was customers like the Williams that paid and kept the status quo. We hardly ever paid and it wasn't a problem. The wheels of industry kept turning anyway.

What I am coming to is that they had their milk delivered by Brian, and they even had orange juice, too. And bread and eggs. I didn't like stealing from them— they were nice people. I used to do a lot of errands for them and I hardly ever charged them for it, so I almost paid for it that way. It wasn't just for me. It wasn't greed. I had never had orange juice delivered. I stole a few bottles, but never had it legally. The milk we did have was never pasteurised— it was sterilised. It was milk without the cream. To make it last, it was watered down fifty-fifty. It was disgusting.

It was all we had though, and something is better than nothing, right? Well, nearly.

7

The Birmingham Bombings and the Greatest Pram

ON NOVEMBER 21, 1974, BOMBS WERE PLACED IN two city centre pubs: the Mulberry Bush and the Tavern in the Town. I watched the whole episode from my bathroom window.

I was sitting on my bathroom windowsill, looking at the bright lights of the town centre, wondering about the glorious things that might happen there. On this particularly cold winter's evening, I was huddled up in my pyjamas when there was a huge explosion. The sound carried across the night sky. We lived only three kilometres from the city centre, so the noise reached me quickly. Within minutes the ambulances and fire engines raced by. Dozens of police cars quickly followed.

I had no idea, of course, what had gone on— only that it was something big. I sat there for a few more minutes and then there was a second explosion. The place was in mayhem.

I ran into the lounge and found the door to the balcony open. My parents were on the balcony, watching the same scene. I turned the telly on and pushed the button for

BBC 1.

The problem had reached the media, and there was a newsflash. It stated that there had been an explosion in a pub, and it was suspected that it was a bomb. At that point they got the news that a second bomb had gone off and that the police had received a phone call from a man with an Irish accent, telling them that there was a bomb, but they hadn't found it in time.

In the coming days it was realised that twenty-one people died and one hundred and eighty-two were injured. The backlash received by the Irish community was horrendous. Everybody was a bomber. Young kids, mothers and, especially, teenage boys and men, were suspects. Irish women were being searched in the town and the prams were probed with the babies still in them.

I have never fought as much in my life as this period of time. All the Irish community suffered just as the innocent Muslim communities during and after the 9/11 tragedy. Of course, the media coverage was less then, but the effect of it was quite real. I fought every day in school; on the way home from school. All the people in our grove suffered the same thing. Innocent Irish people were being beaten up. Lynch mobs roamed the streets, asking people if they were Irish or supported the IRA. This was a time of uncertainty and the police had to act quickly. Things were out of control and the public were crying for justice. They found that justice was to be quicker than quick when the police arrested six men. They were all jailed in 1975, and received a sentence of life imprisonment. Things started to slow down on the vigilante front and the public were happy. The police had acted swiftly to take down the threat of terrorism, and the people involved had been jailed— later to be released on shaky evidence and awarded compensation for their troubles.

Of course, apart from the troubles I had with the IRA

and the abuse, I still had to get through every day with my home life. I felt I was eight going on thirty. My life had been so full already and was going to get fuller.

Again I was sitting on the bathroom windowsill, looking out of the window. About one hundred metres from my house was the busy Coventry Road. As the name suggests, it runs from Coventry to the centre of Birmingham. It was a late night and I was just about to retire. Sounds posh, doesn't it? 'Just about to retire.' I sound sixty-four. Anyway, I was just about to go to bed when I heard a commotion by the road— shouting and stuff. My ears pricked and I could just see a couple of skinheads walking down the hill towards the Lodge pub. In the opposite direction, a punk rocker was walking. As they got closer something was said and just as they were about to pass, a bus from the garage came hurtling down the hill. As they passed each other, one of the skinheads pushed the punk rocker right under the bus. He was killed instantly and the skinheads ran away. I don't think they were caught, but I know that one of the skinheads killed him. I saw it. That whole episode gave me nightmares for weeks. I was traumatised.

I told my dad, but he said I just imagined it. Only reiterating the fact that no matter what I said I would never be believed. They never believed a word I said. I let it go just like most things.

I tried to console myself within the company of my friends and the pictures. There was a picture house, not to far away from where I lived— later to become the Kingston bingo, where my mom dreamt away her days. On Saturday mornings, there used to be films on.

We used to go across and one person used to pay in. There was a fire exit at the back of the cinema and before even the advertisements came on, the place had four more kids sitting in seats we hadn't paid for. Occasionally, we would get caught, but most of the time we got away with it.

Alongside the picture house was a piece of waste ground where the council allowed the gypsies to set up camp. This was also near the back road to the football ground. More than once I stole a pushchair from the gypsies. I feel that they have cursed me and as soon as I drop a pushchair back, my life will improve. Well, a few times I got caught, and the punishment was this: they used to get a lad the same size, or just a bit bigger, and we would fight. Not just fight, but be strapped together with belts so there was no way you could get away. I was actually very quick and as soon as the buckle was clasped, I was in. Sometimes it worked; sometimes it didn't. I won some, I lost more. One thing I did get from the gypsies was respect, apart from a thick lip. I don't know if this was normal practice or something they did with pram thieves. I have never been strapped together since, but it was all experience on the ladder of life. I also got a fantastic pram once, from which I built the go-cart of the century. A great, big old-fashioned pram with solid wheels. I stripped it down so I just had the axle and wheels left and then attached them to my swag carrier. It was extremely quick, so I had to fit a brake on the side. The very brake Seamus tampered with and almost killed me.

Coventry Road, from the bus garage down to the traffic lights, just before the climb to the bridge by the canal, the pavement was probably three hundred metres long on the opposite side of the road to where we lived. On this side, it was probably one hundred and fifty metres long, because of adjoining roads. The go-cart gang obviously went down the longest stretch of road to get up plenty of speed. It was a time trial, and I was always looking to get an extra kilometre per hour out of the go-cart. On these days, the box came off the back, and the tools were returned to the toolbox in the airing cupboard. It was like Formula One. I used to sit in a black bin liner in summer to lose a few pounds, just for the race.

Anyway, the day came, and we sat at the top of the hill. The timer was set. Away I went. I kicked like a crazy man, jumped on, and I was flying. The wind was rushing through my afro, which wasn't really aerodynamic, and I'm sure it lost me a few seconds. However, at the time, it didn't matter much, as I felt like Jackie Stewart. I travelled the whole length of track, and pulled the brake just at the last minute, before the traffic lights. Seamus had, however, cut through the brake just enough so I wouldn't notice, but knew damn well it wouldn't hold under any pressure whatsoever. The brake snapped, and I just kept going, narrowly missing a car. I hit the kerb on the other side and took off— my red afro and the cheesecloth shirt blowing in the wind. For a few seconds, I looked like the human shuttlecock. I was travelling in slow motion. It didn't last long before I was brought back to earth, literally, with a bump. I hit the ground, landing on my afro, which cushioned the fall, skidding on my back along the pavement. My shirt was in ribbons. I looked like I had had a fight with a lion. I didn't win.

A small part of my afro was on the ground, where I had made contact with it, and there was a huge hole in the bum of my side pockets. The go-cart had somersaulted and landed only centimetres from my auburn crash hat. The wheels had buckled beyond recognition and the body had almost split in two. My friends ran down after witnessing the whole scene from the top of the hill, and thought I was dead. However, this was not the case and I was already thinking how I would take my revenge on cock-eyed, when I returned home.

Meanwhile, I shifted the afro a little to cover the patch that was in my hand and hobbled home with my go-cart dragging behind me. It was wrecked. It went from the greatest pram to the greatest go-cart, to the greatest near-death experience I ever had.

8

Dixon Road School

Dixon Road School— fantastic times

THE SCHOOL I WENT TO DURING THIS TIME WAS a Victorian-built school that was full of promise and wonder. I followed my older brother and sister there and the reputation they had, haunted me for quite a while. There were fantastic teachers though, and the food was just delicious. School dinners. The kids used to complain about the school dinners, but I thought they were great. Roast beef with all the trimmings, shepherd's pie, and cauliflower cheese. The list was endless. For pudding, there was spotted dick, banana custard and, of course, chocolate concrete. The person who invented chocolate should have a knighthood or a dame-ship or whatever it's called. Pure genius. They have made so many school kids so happy over the years.

On my first day, I was shepherded to Mr. Evans' class. A Welsh man, don't you know. He was a great teacher and very smart. Old-school type. He sat me next to Andrew Smart and Frank Delaney. It would turn out to be a long-lasting friendship with both children. Andrew was a good lad and he had an older brother, Martin. They lived close to the school with their father. He was a steward at the club my dad used to go to. He had a big shoe, meaning he had one leg shorter than the other and they built up his shoe. You don't see that anymore. He used to rule the house with a rod of iron, ex-army type. I remember he was very smart. Always clean shaven, silver hair short back and sides, slicked back with Brylcreem. He always wore a shirt and tie and a blazer. He looked after the kids alone. Andrew was just a smaller version of his dad— very smart and always clean, with his hair slicked back. The first time I met Andrew's dad, he told me to get a haircut. He did a good job with Andrew. Martin was a wild one.

Frank Delaney, on the other hand, had a very tough time. He was also a great lad. Jet black teeth, and far poorer than us. He didn't have clean clothes from one week to the next. I liked him.

Despite all his problems, Frank had a great sense of humour. He never stopped laughing whilst he was at school. He had such a strong character. His home life was horrendous. He had a father who was drunk all the time. I used to walk him home since some of the kids picked on him because he had it bad.

"Poor little mite." The rich kids, that was.

They didn't have a clue what was going on behind

closed doors. I remember one time I hit him because he was just getting on my nerves. Just playground stuff. He broke down. He cried so hard and for so long and at the end of it he just sat there with his face in his hands, sat on the step in the schoolyard. Eventually, when I got him to stop, I told him I was sorry a few times and gave him some chocolate.

He then looked up and said, "Please don't hit me,Christian; not you, too."

That solitary sentence absolutely floored me. I was crying myself and turned away briefly from his frail, skinny face. The dark shadows under his eyes told their own story. It was from that moment forward I vowed no one would hit Frank again. This kid was seven, maybe eight, and he had had so much suffering in those short years to last a lifetime. No one in school hit Frank again. Even when he got into trouble and was going to get the cane, I stood up and said it was me and took it for him. I didn't know how I was going to do it, but I fought everyone who came close to Frank. He was like a little brother to me. He took me home a few times and I have never seen deprivation like that to this day. It was so bad that it has stayed with me for thirty-six years. As if it was yesterday.

The first time he took me home, he said, "Please, Christian, don't tell the others at school."

I promised I wouldn't. Frank turned the key in the door, and we went inside. As soon as one foot was on the threshold, the smell hit you. Frank lived with his little sister, who Frank had looked after most of the time, because his dad was drunk. His mother had gone years before.

The whole place was like a Dickens novel. The hall had never been cleaned. I mean never. There was grime and dirt thick on the floor, cobwebs hanging off everything and litter, old shoes and clothes all over the floor. We went through to the lounge and the same thing there. The place was freezing, and it was Frank's job to light the fire and get some food for himself. I helped him light the fire, and then went to the kitchen. All that was there was an old piece of bread. I mean it had mould on it. Frank scraped the mould off it, took it back to the fire and toasted it there. When it was done he ate it. No butter, no nothing. That was all he was going to get that evening. I saw him the next day and asked him what he had for breakfast. He said he never ate breakfast because, if he did, he wouldn't have any dinner. I just stood there. I'm not sure if you are supposed to have empathy at eight years old, but I have never felt so sorry for anybody in all my life, so far. I actually thought— no, knew— that he had it far worse than me. I made sure Frank never went hungry again. Everything I had, I gave him half. Everything I didn't have, I gave him half. All the scams I did, Frank got something out of it. I was tied. I couldn't abandon him. He had nothing. I had a bit more than nothing, but it was more than him. In school we were inseparable. Outside school my hands were tied. I would walk him home and watch him go in the front door to his terraced house. When the door was closed he was by himself. Well, him and his sister and his so-called dad. I wondered what his father thought of the word 'Dad'. How he perceived the job. Was the role of dad to him just being in the same house? Or did he think his job was done once the kids were born. I did not know Frank's dad, so I do not know what he thought. I would, however, like to turn the clock back and ask him straight out. I would probably get a thick lip for talking to an elder that way. It is quite strange that it doesn't really matter how an elder behaves; you still, as a child, have to respect them. In my book, you earn respect. You are not given it through fear. I read in a biography of Sidney Poitier that the measure of a man is judged by the way he raises his children. I wonder what Mr. Delaney would have thought about that.

Mr. Evans, my class teacher, in the meantime, wasn't frightened to push boundaries. In one particular science lesson, he told us that it was going to be extra special. That we were going to learn about the body. I was always interested in anatomy and medicine so my ears pricked up immediately. The week before, we were allowed to dissect a frog. That was fascinating stuff. Sandra Geary almost threw up and Marlene Warden held my hand to steady herself. I loved science, I really did. If I could have held Marlene's hand in every lesson, that would have been something.

"So, boyo, what do you think of that?" Mr. Evans asked, looking at me with a glint in his eyes.

I said it was great and couldn't wait to see what he had up his sleeve.

Mr. Evans brought a container to the table, and we all gathered around. He took the lid off and there, looking at us, were a dozen sheep eyes. A few girls screamed and took steps back, trying to get away from that 'elusive enemy'. Most of the boys stepped forward, shouting, "Great! Wicked!"

Mr. Evans told us that we had to pair up and we would get an eye each. We had to dissect it and take a look at how the eye worked. He scrolled down the board. There was an intricate drawing of the eye. We had to identify all the workings of the eye and that was going to be the class work and homework for the next few days. I loved it. I did this great elaborate folder with all the drawings I had done of what goes where, how the information travels into the brain and where it goes to. I got a gold star for the work and was delighted. I actually thought that I liked this school lark. You get praise for something you do right and a tap on the back when you get things wrong. I could handle that.

My time for the most part in school was most enjoyable. There was the odd run-in with Mr. Jarvis, of course, and, when you heard him coming down the corridors, kids just scattered.

On the heels of his shoes he had tips, and when you heard the *click, click, click* on the concrete floor, your world just came to an end. You knew you were in trouble even when you didn't do anything. Mother Theresa would have jumped the fence when Mr. Jarvis showed up. He was absolutely terrifying.

My whole time at school was mainly based around the dinner bell. I loved school dinners until my run-in with Frank— then it was just once you went up, because Frank was getting fatter by the day. He was even taking food home for his sister. He used to tuck it under his jumper when no one was looking. A fruit scone fell out of his jumper once on the way out of the dining hall, and Mr. Jarvis grabbed him and dragged him off to his office. I followed, of course, to hear him giving Frank a right old bellyful. I ran into the office and told him what was going on at Frank's home. I said he wasn't stealing anything and that it was my food that I didn't want.

At the end of a fifteen-minute discussion, Frank and I just sat there as Mr. Jarvis took notes.

We were then dismissed, and Frank was allowed to keep the food. It was the only time that we got away with anything. The next day, Frank said someone had been around to the house and asked his dad lots of questions. He didn't know what the outcome was, so we just left it at that. Frank then moved away, and I don't know what happened to him. I was sad for a long time, and wonder to this day what happened to him. Frank, if you're out there, call me, Christian.

There were other fantastic teachers at the school, too. There was Mr. Scott who later became my form teacher. Heavy set and a little chubby. Well, actually a lot chubby. However, I think he could forgive me for that. I pushed way too often, and then he used to just explode. He had hands like dustbin lids and used them occasionally. He introduced me to the Beatles as he used to play them all the time in class. He was also the school football team manager and, of course, I played at the back with another kid called Abdul. Mr. Scott saved my life when I slipped on some wet grass and landed flat on my back. I was chewing gum at the time and it got stuck in my throat. Mr. Scott belted me on the back with his mighty paw and out it flew. I thanked him mightily then and I will do it again now. Thanks, Mr. Scott, you were a star. Hopefully, he will read it himself now that the book has been published.

Abdul was a big lad. There was no way he was eight or nine. He had a great, thick moustache and pubic hair. What the bloody hell was that all about? I didn't have a clue, but he stayed in the team and was an absolute star. A nice kid, too.

Mrs. Jackson was one who took a real shine to me and treated me like a long lost son. She used to take me ice skating on Saturdays for a long time. She used to pick me up in her sports car and take me to town where she lived. We used to have tea and buns, and would then go ice skating. Wonderful woman. She was great in school, too. I could do nothing wrong with her. I really thought that it would last forever. I remember messing up big time, and can't quite remember what I did, but she was none too happy. She was really disappointed in me and so that was that.

Miss Peal was absolutely gorgeous and I had a real crush on her. She used to come real close and I could smell her perfume. Every now and then, when walking through a department store or something, I get the same whiff and I'm straight back with Miss Peal. Fabulous teacher with the perfect teaching personality. She was also my form teacher later, which I absolutely loved.

Mr. Francombe— he was really cool. He wore corduroy the whole time and had a Citroen. A bright red one. He looked like a mix between Gilbert O'Sullivan and Art Garfunkel. He could play the guitar and got that out almost every day. As I said earlier, these people became my role models. They were the people I looked up to every day, and I was always quite sad when the school holidays came, because I wouldn't see them for eight weeks.

Mr. Barber was the deputy head teacher. He also was in charge of the choir and Mr. Scott, God bless him, had put my name forward for the choir. I was absolutely petrified, but did it anyway. I had to stand and sing in front of the choir like an audition. I can't remember what I sang, but I know it was ropey. I got in anyway and have been singing every day since. There I was introduced to the other school choir members. Amongst them were twins named Sylvester and Cyril Washington. They were Jamaican— sorry, that was a little obvious, wasn't it? Not many Chinese with the name Sylvester. Sylvester Wing? I don't think so. Eventually, we became good friends, and we sang a lot together. They introduced me to the gospel choir in their Methodist church. I was already going to church and that didn't interest me at all. To listen to this hypocrisy, even then, was just mind-numbing. Everything you did, you did for God. If you didn't put enough money in the box, God would be watching and you would be punished accordingly. I remember sitting in church with my parents, and they came around with the begging box. I remember the Father telling me to think hard before I put my money in, as God was watching me and I didn't want to go to Hell now, did I? Well that was all the fuel I needed.

I asked him, "It's supposed to be warm in Hell, right?"

He said it was.

I then said, "So God watches over our every move, right?"

He said he did.

I then said that he watches us freeze every winter. He said he does, he watches our every move. I then said that I'm not putting in any money then, because Hell sounds like a great place. A lot warmer, anyway.

Well, my mom froze, and my dad started sniggering. The priest put his hand up to slap me, and my dad said that he would be one step closer to god if he put one finger on me.

The priest continued, visibly shaken by what had happened.

Well, as you can imagine, me and the Catholic Church never saw eye to eye. It just didn't wash with me. My mom was mortified when I told her I didn't want to go and, every time she mentioned it, I would protest in some way or another. She was horrified when I told her I wanted to be a Rastafarian. I seemed to fit in the Gospel church and it worked for me. She told my dad, and she said that maybe I was hanging around with Protestants and I would come around. I never did. My brothers and sisters still went to church, but I always got away with it.

The singing was always good, but I never wanted to be a choir boy. It just didn't seem right that I didn't believe in God but sang in his house, praising Him. No, it wasn't for me.

Mr. Barber, the choir master in school, was brilliant for me. He would introduce the classics to me and that was just amazing. I still can't sing like Pavarotti, but I have a good go. He gave us hymn sheets all the time to learn the words and I had a cunning plan for those.

Sylvester, Cyril and I, got together one evening and said that maybe we could take our singing skills on the road. Of course, I immediately thought of Broadway, the bright lights.

New York, New York. And if I can't make it ...

No. Sylvester brought me down to earth with a bang. He suggested we sing in the local pubs at Christmas time. I would go in and ask the landlord if we could sing some Christmas carols for the punters. Which would get them in the Christmas spirit and then they would drink more. Quite simple, really.

Most of the time the landlord agreed. We would go in and sing four or five carols and then Cyril would walk around with his beret and the punters would put in a few coppers. We would do this for a solid month, right the way through December and all the proceeds would be split three ways. One year was very good. We earned eighty-five pounds in the month, which were twenty-eight pounds and thirty-three pence each. Mind you, we *earned* it. We used to walk for kilometres in the freezing cold and go from pub to pub. Thinking back, it was actually quite dangerous, and we got chased a few times. Running on the snow or ice with pockets full of change is not easy, but it was worth it. At the end of the evening, we used to go to our local fish and chip shop and order curry and chips in a tray. It was twelve pence. A real luxury at the end of the night, I can tell you. My singing continued after Christmas and I still went to the Methodist churches for a long time. I really enjoyed it. Yes, the theme wasn't the best for me, but we enjoyed ourselves. That was the point.

9

Pontin's— The Great British Holiday

EVERY YEAR, THE ARMY SENT US TO PONTIN'S HOLIDAY camp in Rhyl. For anyone who is unfamiliar with the Pontin's holiday theme, it is this: a cheap holiday — basic, yet clean, accommodation in chalets. It had one or two bedrooms and a kitchenette— that French-sounding word again.

Everything was on a single camp-style site, without tents.

Entertainment was in the main ballroom, where there was a large bar and, of course, good value for money. There was a restaurant with good, basic food. Of course, you are catering for the working class, so no French muck here, oh no. There were staff members who would cater for your every need and keep the kids thoroughly entertained for the duration of the stay. One or two weeks, depending on which working class you were— poor working class or posh working class. We, of course, were poor, part-time working class, so we got one week.

Rhyl is not Benidorm and it isn't Greece, either. It is a popular tourist destination and is situated on the north east coast of Wales. Because the army was paying, bless their souls, they obviously didn't pick the most expensive time of the year. They picked April or May. Now we all know that they are not the sunniest months and if you know Wales, you know what the weather might be doing that time of year.

Rain, rain and, guess what, more bloody rain. One week in the rain. However, as I said earlier, all the entertainment was for free and, if I wasn't in the cinema watching Abbot and Costello, I would be playing table tennis or snooker. It was great, actually. One week in the rain in Rhyl sure beats one week in Birmingham. The accommodation was great. Basic, but warm and cosy. I didn't wet the bed too often and that was a holiday in itself. To wake up dry was a time for celebration— a big glass of water, I think, as I wasn't allowed to drink after seven in the evening. We had the time of our lives at Pontin's. The donkey derby, where I always had the donkey that was due for retirement, or the one with three legs, or which was nailed to the ground. It never moved a bloody millimetre.We went every year for about five years. I'm sure it was the same donkey and they only brought the thing out when I came. Lightning bolt, I think it was called. A lightning bolt was what it needed.

There was the boat lake. That's where you had two- and four-seater pedal boats of different colours on a lake that was only thirty centimetres deep. At one time, they made you wear life vests.

On a two-year-old the water only went to the knees. Bloody life vest indeed. The knobbly knees competitions, where I was always entered and actually came third once. An old woman beat me into a second place and a human x-ray came first. Then there was the swimming in the sea. That was Hell on Earth, too. It was always freezing cold, and the beach at the water's edge was like quicksand. I used to have these swimming trunks that were made of a wool type material that quickly turned into a hula skirt as soon as it touched the water. My willy disappeared like a tortoise's head as soon as *that* hit the water. If you went out too far, the skirt would drag me under the water. I needed a rubber ring two metres from the water's edge, just in case.

I remember one year we arrived at Pontin's on the Saturday at around 2 p.m. after catching the train from New Street Station— with my boiled sweets in hand. I had to have them for travel sickness. I even got sick on my bike— I was useless. Anyway, as I said, we arrived around 2 p.m., with all the hopes and dreams of a good holiday. Mom and Dad had managed to save a little bit of money— since the army had paid for the holiday, it would be a bit cheeky to ask for spending money, too. So they had a bit of cash and we checked into the room as normal and grabbed the key with a great big piece of wood attached so you wouldn't lose it. You could kill someone with that key, but they would always find the murder weapon.

It was always my job to look after the key. I could barely carry the thing to the chalet, which was a three-mile trek with my suitcase, my sweets, and my Dandy. I needed a holiday when I got there. It took two people to open the door.

So anyway again, sorry, we arrived on the Saturday and we went mad. I had a bit of money saved from my various schemes, of which you know about. I had that all spent by 5 p.m. Bloody arcades. They have been the ruin of many a young boy. Especially the machine where you put the two-pence piece in, hit a board with steel pegs and fall onto a flat-bed, which was pushing backwards and forwards at a snail's pace. On the flat-bed were other two penny pieces that had joined together and looked like one great, big huddle. They would go right near the edge as the flat-bed pushed forward and retreat again as the flat-bed moved backwards. My hope was that my two pence would push his way into the group and then, as the flat-bed moved forward, the gathering would fall off the edge and into the tray where I could collect my bounty. Yippee!

I pushed my two pence in delicately, thinking that would make a difference, and I held my breath and waited and waited and waited... *Crap!* It had just joined the other group for a jolly old singsong.

"Christian is a loser! Christian is a loser!"

Three pounds later, I was done and thoroughly miserable. *What a crap holiday this is going to be*, I thought. I went to join the outlaws and see if I could get some more money. No joy. They had a budget, and were only allowed to spend three pounds a day. That was for beer, for bingo and, oh yes, food. Pontin's was cheap, but that was really pushing it.

Three pounds a day. What's that all about? You mean we have come on holiday and we have to struggle again for everything? This can't be right. Everybody else is having a jolly old time and we budget?

Mom and Dad were stone broke by Monday. Well, almost. We had ninety-seven pence left— so much for budgeting. They had blown the lot on drink and cigarettes, and, oh yes, food. We had five days to go before we go home. I was starving hungry and was planning a sortie to the cafeteria: operation 'pinch as much as you can and run like mad'.

It was survival now. I was even going to make friends with the nerd next door, flash my big cow eyes and the mother would fall in love with me, take pity and feed me like the lost soul I pretended to be. That was Plan B. Mom came up with Plan C.

"Maybe, just maybe, I could try me luck at the bingo."

This did not go down too well with any of us. Mom had never won at bingo. Never. Never ever. However, all the protests went in vain. She talked my dad around after bringing him a couple of pints first from the bar, and us some crisps and pop, and headed away with her customary 'wish me luck'.

We weren't hopeful. History had proven itself to be a sorrowful time, and why should now be any different? We played cards and an hour later she came home looking a bit sad.

"Well?" my dad asked.

"Nah, no luck."

"What a surprise!" we all shouted.

One after the other, we said what we had to say, and got clouted for being a bit loud, and that was that. We were going home early. The only holiday I got and we are going home bloody early. Not only that, but what do I tell my pals at home? We came home early because we ran out of money? Not bloody likely. I might be poor and desolate, smell and wet the bed, but pride I have. No sir, I would hate to lie through my teeth, but it had to be good. Really good.

Dad beat up the security guard after one too many... Plausible. Mom had another baby, which was stolen... Immaculate conception... Three day pregnancy... Not plausible. I got caught stealing food... a car... money for food or car... Plausible. I broke into the Pontin's safe and got caught with the loot... Plausible. We entered Seamus in the under seventeen's beauty contest for girls and was disqualified for not being the only one with a moustache, but the thickest... Plausible.

It was hopeless. What could I think of that would be believable?

Mom, meanwhile, started rummaging around in her handbag. This was not un-common— she would always try to see if she could find a coin or two in the lining.

"Just in case," she'd say.

Well, anyway, I was watching her out the corner of my eye and, very slowly, she put a great big wad of notes on the table top, closed her purse, and said absolutely nothing.

There was absolute silence. Dad stopped mid slurp. I stopped mid thought. Seamus stopped mid picking his nose and Martha stopped mid looking in the mirror.

Mom still said nothing. I was the first to rise to take it and was the last to take it. God, Dad was quick when he needed to be. The whole lot was in his fist and back to his lap whilst the pint was hanging in mid air and held again. Seamus fell over his Noddy Holder shoes and almost broke an ankle, and Martha nearly poked her eye out with the hairbrush. I was on the floor in melee with my big ginger afro in tatters.

"How much did you win?" my dad asked, with his film star good looks.

"One hundred pounds," my mom said, with here radio star good looks.

My dad toothed his immaculate smile and said, "Come on, let's party."

We did just that. Anything we wanted, we had. We were spoilt rotten and it felt good. Reality was not all it was cracked up to be. It was great being rich. We spent the rest of the week living the way normal people live. Or how it was perceived by us then. 'Normal'— what a laugh!

Anyway, it was great, and I felt like a king. A rather smelly, trampy, gingered afro type of king, but a king all the same. Martha felt like a queen and Seamus too. No, not a typo.

We went home, and then it hit me: we would never have a holiday like that again.

10

The First Time It Happened

WHEN I WAS AROUND SEVEN, I MET SOMEONE WHOM I will call 'Neighbour Y', since 'Y' seems to be the perfect letter and question. He was on the fringe of the larger group of kids. I will call him Y because of legal reasons, but, if this book goes to print, I will find this bastard and expose him for what he was then, and probably still is. He was around fourteen or fifteen, and his parents were well respected. He was a loner and sadist. He used to get his pellet gun and shoot cats and dogs, and basically whatever he could get in his sights. He never really got on with the other kids— he was just too different. He used to do models and stuff, and thought he was a Kung Fu Jimmy. As you know, this was the period of Bruce Lee and *Enter the Dragon*. Every kid in our neighbourhood wanted to be Bruce Lee. *Kung Fu* was on every Sunday, and the kids used to go in for the show, and then go back out again— if their parents would let them, because Sunday night was bath night.

Anyway, everybody was crazy about Kung Fu and martial arts in general, and neighbour Y was no different. I used to go in his house, and we would practice moves and stuff. He was a bit rough, but I was a tough kid, so I took it on the chin. He was also quite wealthy and had all the latest martial arts gear. I was jealous of all the stuff he had and wished I had it, too. It was difficult not to. He was a bit nerdy, but a bit cool, as well, if you know what I mean.

One day, I said I really liked his tracksuit top— a gold and black front zip-up with a dragon on the back. It was really cool. He said I could have it if I did something for him. I said I would do anything for him, no problem. He said okay, and went around the back of me and pulled down my trousers and pants. I didn't know what the hell was going on. He then told me that it wouldn't hurt, and penetrated me. He kept going until he ejaculated— maybe for a few minutes. I didn't know what that meant then, but I know what the outcome was. He had held me close during the rape, and every now and then I can still smell him. His cologne drifts in and is picked up by the memory of that fateful day. I still smell him.

Then he just pulled my trousers and pants back up, and we continued our Kung Fu session. I was in shock. I had no idea what had happened. It hurt like hell. He had lied about that, and the strangest thing of all was that I felt embarrassed and ashamed about the whole sordid act. I knew what he had done was wrong, but how was I going to tell people what had happened? They would never believe me anyway— that's what Neighbour Y had said.

"They will never believe you."

If he had done it to other kids, I don't know. I was eight.

I said that I had to go home, and he threw the top at me. He said that I had earned it and maybe we should do it again some time. I did not do it again any time. Something like this you just kept quiet about because of the stigma attached. I kept it quiet, and never went around to his house again. I never went near him again, and, when I saw his parents in the street, I ducked my head. I was ashamed. I felt dirty.

In time, the pain of the act went away and things became normal again. I was never the same again. I know it. How I would have grown up without that experience, I don't know. The trust had gone for everybody. I trusted no one. Everybody looked different to me. They would never be the same again. Nothing was the same again. I actually never wore the top either— it reminded me too much of that day. I left it in the cupboard. It was tainted.

At the start of the chapter I said the first time it happened. The next time I was abused was by a scout master, named scout leader Y. This happened about a year later. Again, for legal reasons, he was Y. On the surface he was a normal, everyday guy. He was just a little too fond of young boys, if you know what I mean. Well anyway, he would target a boy and then groom him. He would tell them that they were great at this and great at that. He knew what he was doing. He always targeted the inner city kids. The ones where the parents didn't have much money and the kids were a burden and not really loved or cared for. He was a hunter, a predator. This was probably the first time they had ever been told that they had ever been good at anything. You could see them glow. It was brilliant for them. He did it to me after a series of these kids had just left the group unexpectedly. He said that they had moved to another scout group, or made some excuse that seemed plausible at the time. Of course, I didn't trust him or anything he said. Yet, he still got to me. It happened so quickly that I didn't really know what was going on. After class one evening, he asked me if I could help him clean up. I said yes. He hadn't tried anything before, so I didn't think much of it. He was a real joker, and he made me laugh a lot. I liked him.

So, at the end, he said thanks and I turned away. He grabbed me from behind and started hugging me really hard. That was it the first time, but things got progressively worse and, when he asked me to help him clean after the fifth or sixth class, I knew that this would probably be the worst one yet, as history had presented itself. I was a bit wary, so I said I couldn't, and he said that he had to rush home and could do with a volunteer then. No one came forward. He said it wasn't good that no one had come forward, and that we would have to stay over until somebody did. It wasn't fair that he should do it all by himself, and we were a scout troupe and should help each other. So he asked me again. The other lads were pushing me forward, so I said okay, I would do it. The minute the door was bolted behind the last of the kids, he was on me. It took me quite by surprise. He grabbed me from behind, and again I tried to pull away. I felt his erection on my bum and tried to pull away, but he said that he was just saying thank you and was just giving me a hug. I said okay. Then he started rubbing me with his hand and continued to rub my bum with his erection. Then he groaned and moved away. I felt really uncomfortable. He said that he had to check the bathroom, and disappeared. I just stood there, again confused.

A few minutes later, he came out and acted as if nothing had happened.

He said, "Thanks again for your help, and see you next time."

I said, "Yeah sure."

Then I went. I didn't live too far from the hut, so I walked home. I would never return. Again, I felt dirty and ashamed. What the bloody hell was going on? Was this normal? Can people do this when they want? I was totally confused and asked my school mates indirectly about this sort of thing. They said they hadn't had this, and that I should just go to the police. I hadn't had the best times with them, so I just let it go. A few years later, I saw him driving a bus. It stopped at a traffic light. I walked across and glanced at the driver. It was him. I couldn't believe it. I just stopped and stared. I don't know if he recognised me, but I knew him. The bus pulled away, and I never saw him again.

The next time I was abused was a more prolonged affair. This lasted a few years, and I don't really know why I let it go on for so long. Actually, I do.

Once again, the grooming. "They will never believe you."

The usual things. Nothing new. All normal. Wasn't it?

The problem was that this offender was also a relative. An uncle, in fact. Uncle. He would often stay with us because he had nowhere else to go. He was a charming, handsome man at the time and had his pick of the women. He was well built and really didn't have any problem with the opposite sex. He used to take me to play pool at the age of about nine or ten. You could get into the pubs in those days if you kept quiet and kept your head down. So Uncle Y and I used to play pool, and he would buy me pop and crisps. I liked him— he was a free spirit. He was cool. Even though I was young I had already learnt that something will always cost. If you get something for free, you always pay for it somehow. I did.

Because we were poor, the couch we had was no good for sleeping on. So I had to share my bed with him. Me at the bottom, and him at the top. The first time we went out, there was no problem at all. Well, I don't think so, anyway— I fell asleep quite quickly. What happened whilst I was asleep, I have no idea. God knows. So it became a regular thing. Each time he visited, he would stay with us and we would play pool. He would then stay in my bed. It all changed one evening when we returned from the pub. I got undressed, down to my pants, and jumped into bed. Uncle Y got into bed and the lamp went out. The next thing, I felt a hand around my groin. I panicked and just froze. He then climbed out of the bed and got into bed at my end. He then asked me what I thought about playing with his thing. I said I didn't want to. He said that if I want to continue going to the pub to play pool and eat crisps, I had better do what he told me to. He put my hand on his penis and told me to pull it up and down. I did what he told me to. I didn't have any choice. He said that he would tell my mom and dad that I said I would do it for money. When he was finished, he turned over and went to sleep. I just laid there, again in turmoil.

This happened for a few years— every time he came to stay— until, one day, I said that if he didn't get away from me I would tell my dad. He said that he wouldn't believe me. I told him I would take my chances, and gave him to three to get away. I counted, and, at the last second, he moved away. He never came to stay with us again. He actually never came to the house again, and always made excuses every time he was invited. I heard later that he had died of cancer. It was a long, slow death. What goes around comes around, right?

Author's Note

I THINK THE EXPERIENCE OF THIS ABUSE HAS MADE ME into the person I am today. I think without these happenings I would not have had the strength and resolve that has become the make-up of my personality. I do wish I could turn the clock back and to not have it happen, but it did. I can't change that. However, what I could do is break the circle and move forward. That is exactly what I did. I was having a second go at life at ten years old. I had to.

Nothing was ever going to break me and nothing was ever going to beat me. I was determined to get through anything that was thrown at me. Anything. I also realised much later, that it was not my fault and I was not to blame.

The thing is, you carry around the shame, the guilt and the sordid secret wherever you go. It is with you every day of your life. You never forget it and you never really forgive the people that did this to you. Each day that passes you just deal with it better, until there actually comes a time when you can let your sordid little secret out. With that goes the shame of what happened and the guilt of what happened. You can actually talk about it and that becomes the therapy to the burden you have carried for so long. It is freeing. It is liberating. It allows you now, finally, to live. You will, however, never get the years back that were stolen from you so violently. Never. There are people who never recover from this type of violence and worse. They are always trapped in it. They remain the victim. I am, as it happens, one of the lucky ones. I am able to move on and live a 'normal' life.

Of course, I am not the same as everyone else who was not abused. I am scarred. I am an over-sensitive, emotional wreck at times, and a compulsive face reader. Every situation I get into I read the face and react accordingly. I face things head on and am absolutely impulsive and a risk taker. Would I have it any other way? I'm not sure. It has made my life interesting. That much I'm sure of. At times, I wish I could have relaxed in situations and thought a bit of the consequences, but, as I said, you carry around the legacy of the abuse and you are acting within the realms of this. You become a reactionary. In some shape or form I will always be a victim because of this. The perpetrators have no idea of the long-term affect of abuse— whether it be mental, physical or sexual. Only the innocent victim will know this and hopefully the people who read stories like mine. They will then understand the situation a little better.

11

The Holy Trinity

THE HOLY TRINITY WAS NOT WHAT IT SEEMS.
This place was actually a derelict Gothic church, which was
not very far from where we lived.

The place fascinated me. I loved and at the same time
hated the architecture. It used to frighten me. It was
overbearing. When you stood at the bottom of one of the
pillars and looked up, it felt like the whole building was
falling over you. Enveloping you in this stone glove. I
marvelled at the structure and the skill involved in building
such a place. I walked in the grounds, taking in the whole
atmosphere. It was an intimidating place, but that was the
whole point, wasn't it? To intimidate people into believing
God was great and this is the house of the Lord.

At the back of the church was a great set of arched
double doors, which was where the carriage drove in,
carrying the bodies in earlier years. Here they would unload
the corpse and take them down into the basement, down a
set of steps.

At the end of the graveyard was a huge wall. You
couldn't see the wall because the top was at ground level. I
do not know if, originally, the wall would have been taller,
but they used to bury bodies on top of bodies in the old
days when they ran out of plots. Maybe over time this is

what happened. Beyond the wall, there was a three-metre drop to ground level. I used to climb up this wall to get in the graveyard from the street below. It was the quickest and easiest route. I suppose the graveyard held about three hundred graves. I used to read the headstones. The oldest one I found was 1787. I don't know if this was the oldest, but it was the oldest one I found.

At night time there were never any lights on and of course the whole place would then come alive with wildlife. We used to go up there at the dead of night and dare each other to walk around the churchyard alone. I hated doing that— you felt like you were being watched the whole time. Every shadow, every rustle in the bushes, you thought was someone coming to get you. Or some*thing*. There were bats flying around the church all the time. They would swoop down, and you could feel the flutter of wings brush your face. It was absolutely terrifying.

We did it anyway. One Halloween the whole group got together and set up an extravagant dare.

At the stroke of midnight, the witching hour, we would go to the church with torches, get into the church, and do a séance. What did we know about stuff like that? I'll tell you what we knew about stuff like that: absolutely nothing. However, we went all the same. There were about fifteen kids of various ages. All the parents were out, mostly to the Halloween celebrations.

So getting out at that time was not a problem, especially if you were with older kids.

We all met in the square and lighted our torches. Real torches. Some kids put petrol on theirs, but Chris O'Hara— my hero— found some lamp oil in an old shed and put that on some old rags his mother was selling to the rag and bone man. The torch burnt brilliantly. The petrol torches burnt away very quickly, but the oil torch just kept on going. We set off and looked like a lynch mob out of a

Frankenstein movie. We walked down the back of Chris
O'Hara's house and down the hill to Bordesley Park Road.
Across to the Horse and Jockey pub, and then, a hundred
metres later, past the Plume and Feathers pub, and around
the corner under the Brockhouse Bridge.

Ahead was the church, and I was scared stiff. Going
there during the day was quite bad. At night, it was very
bad. At twelve midnight, the witching hour, on Halloween?
Absolute madness. We scaled the wall to the graveyard, and
we all walked through towards the big double doors. I can
say that I could see nothing. The only torch we had left was
the oil torch, and that was held by Chris at the front of the
group. I was ninth along the line. As we approached the
church, the torch was casting a dull glow against the walls.
The shadows danced across the stonework. Everyone was
silent. I'm sure, at this stage, everyone thought this was a
very bad idea, but we kept going. We walked passed all the
gravestones and finally got to the big double doors and
huddled around, waiting for the orders.

We decided that we would go in one after the other and
then meet inside. The doors were prised open and a stick
pushed between the two to stop them from being closed.
Of course, Chris went inside first and left the rest of us in
the dark. There was a slight panic, and I think it took fifteen
seconds for us all to get inside. The last one in was
panicking like crazy. Not that inside was any better.

The room was about seventy square metres and about
eight metres high, and the light we had was only casting
shadows into the corners. Chris lifted the torch to reveal a
mural of a Union Jack, which was about sixteen square
metres. I think they probably used the place as an air raid
shelter during the war. You could have certainly fitted a few
people in there. We gathered together and were wondering
in truth what the bloody hell we were doing there. It was
absolutely terrifying. I was not happy at all, but pretended

to the rest that I was tough anyway. There was a door in the left hand corner and we decided that we had to explore and that this wasn't the best place for a séance. We headed towards the door, and it was Mark Smith who pushed out his hand and grabbed the door handle. My heart was beating out of my chest. I was waiting for Dracula to appear. Mark pulled on the handle, and the door creaked open. The light twisted around the door to reveal a set of steps and a black hole. Each child got a turn to peer into the abyss. I finally got my chance, and went forward. There were twenty-seven steps. I know this because I counted each one on the way down. Everybody then said that it was best we didn't go down there with only one light. We then agreed that it would be the ultimate if we did. We went down. I was in the middle of the line, and the one at the back was sniffling. I could hear him.

The atmosphere was alive with fear, excitement and the odd smell of damp and decay. The torch disappeared from sight and the one at the back was now crying. We all scuffled in behind the torch and had a look around. We were in the very depths of the church— in the basement where there were coffins lined up along one wall. Six of them— all dusty and just leant against the wall, doing nothing. Well, this was the catalyst for the pandemonium that followed later.

We sat in a ring, and Chris was the first to ask if it was wise to do a séance in this place. I, for one, was already a stone lighter and a little bit smellier, if that was possible. Any more and I would have had a heart attack. I was sweating audibly, and my heart was not far from stopping completely. We agreed that it wasn't the wisest thing we had ever done.

We stood, and then the torch started to fade. I ran for the stairs and someone got in front of me and pushed me back against the coffins. One fell over and landed with a crash, missing me by centimetres. I swear I ran up that stairs like a banshee. I don't think my feet actually trod on one step. I kind of levitated up the staircase— the whole bunch scrambling behind me. I was running in complete darkness and had a vague idea where the doors were. I hit them doing sixty kilometres an hour, and fell backwards— dazed. People were trampling on each other to get out, everybody screaming. The doors were pushed wide open, I think, by Mark, who hit them full speed. Everybody scrambled out into the graveyard, which was absolutely fantastic. It took us half an hour at least to get our breaths back.

It was a slow walk back and all the lads were saying how brave they were. In truth I was just pleased to get out of there. I can say I had nightmares for a long time after that, and still hold the church as the scariest place I have ever been.

12

Bonfire Night, Christmas and New Year's

THERE WERE ALWAYS SCAMS AT BONFIRE NIGHT. IT WAS a time when you could really earn a few coppers if you were cute enough. Firstly, all the lads in the square would gather wood and we would pile it all behind the O'Hara house. It was a good place to have a bonfire, purely because it was right next to the railway line and out of the way of other properties. However, there were a few problems involved in this.

Firstly, as you remember, Kevin O'Hara was a pyromaniac. Secondly, other children from neighbouring estates came and stole it. And thirdly, the weather was always against us and it was a constant problem to keep it dry.

Let's deal with the first problem, shall we? Kevin was a nightmare on bonfire night or the weeks preceding. He would either set fire to it just at the last minute, or he would set fire to it when we just got enough to call it a bonfire— anything that looked like a tee-pee with more than twenty pieces of wood. So then it was a big scramble to find more and that meant a raid on other bonfires in the surrounding neighbourhoods. The best one was on the new estate on the other side of the railway tracks. However, that meant dealing with all the kids on that side, too. I knew a lot of them anyway through Sylvester and Cyril, my singing pals. There were a lot of tough people on the new estate. Warren Thomas was one of them. A really nice guy, but, when crossed, holy crap, he could move. Bernard Smith— a little younger, but handy, too. I would say there were probably thirty kids on the new estate— twice as many as ours. But to be without a bonfire on bonfire night— not a chance. It was a calculated risk. We would go under the cover of darkness and sneak back across the railway track. The calculated risk was that if we didn't get caught stealing the wood and beaten up, we would get knocked down by a train on the way back. We did it anyway. Sometimes we got caught and then I would have to fight my way out. Sometimes I got away with it and got it back to our bonfire. Only once did I nearly get knocked down by the train and it was only the vibration on the track that saved me that day.

It was a very cold, foggy night and the wind on the tracks was severe, so I pulled my shoulders in, pulled my collar up and set to my task. It worked and I was on my way back with a load of wood that I had thrown over the fence on a number of raids. I clambered over the railway track to the other side. You could never see much as there were no lights on the track, so you kept to the rails and stood on the railway sleepers for a safe footing. I kept going for about half a mile and, with the wind coming from in front of me, I couldn't hear a thing. I just dug in and kept going. Every now and then I would look back and check for trains. The problem was that the trains on that side of the track came around a heavy bend, and you wouldn't know they were there until they were a few hundred metres away. I turned and saw nothing. The next thing I know there was a vibration on the track and the sleepers started trembling. I turned and about a hundred metres away was a train bearing down on me. I could now here the sound and it was deafening. The driver hadn't seen me, and there was no horn. I jumped off the track in the nick of time and fell into the cable ditch at the side of the track. The train rumbled by and then it was gone into the distance. I was very close to pushing up the daisies. Suddenly, the bonfire wasn't so important, after all.

The second problem was trying to stop other people stealing it. We would keep watch on it sometimes— camping out in Kevin O'Hara's back garden— and would wait until someone came. Sometimes there would be a few of us and we would play cards and stuff until the early hours, or until we heard something. When you are young and you were camping in a back garden, every noise was a possible wood pincher. So it was normal that you didn't get much sleep. Sometimes the wood would go missing during the day. It would just be gone when you came home from school. I'm not sure if other kids had stolen it or people in the grove for their fires. It had gone, anyway.

The third problem was the weather. We would, at the early stages, cover the wood with plastic or corrugated sheeting, and weigh it down with bricks. However, the problem with that was that the wind would pick up, and it would be gone. The rain would drench the wood the whole time and so, when November 5 came around, we had a horrendous time lighting it.

How we ever got a fire going at all was a miracle, but then it was sheer delight. We would gather our food and head off. We used to put potatoes straight in the base of the fire and cook them. The more posh kids would wrap them in tin foil, but most just threw them and collect them, using sticks when they were cooked. We would then slice them open and fill them with butter or margarine— whatever was available. Sitting around the fire was the greatest thing. We would be completely red-faced and boiling at the front, whilst freezing cold at the back. So I used to turn around and warm my bum occasionally. Heaven.

Of course, with bonfire night, there was also Guy Fawkes. So we used to make a 'guy' out of old clothes and a small football for a face, put it in my go-cart and took it onto Coventry Road. It wasn't just any old rags thrown together— you had to stuff it, too, and make it as realistic as you could. The more realistic the better.

So I would take it on Coventry Road just by the bus station, and wait until an unsuspecting victim would pass by.

You would then ask them, "A penny for the guy, please, sir."

If you were lucky enough, you would get a few coppers for your trouble.

If you went to a lot of trouble making it, they would judge it well and give you a few more. People appreciated it. I remember one year Mom and Dad had gone out, and I was told I had to look after Robbie for a while. This, of course, was a real hindrance, since I had done my guy and was on my way out. So I put Robbie in the pram instead. I dressed him up a bit, gave him a big coat and woolly hat, and had his legs sticking out the end with some thick socks so he wouldn't get cold, and off I went. Most of the time people gave good money and said I had done a good job, but one guy said that he wasn't happy because it wasn't realistic enough. I said to him that you couldn't get any more realistic than actually real, and took the hat off to reveal my little blue-faced brother, who was obviously a little cold. He almost laughed his head off and gave me fifty pence for my cheek. Brilliant. At the end of the evening we went to the chip shop and had some chips. Robbie was delighted and I had a pocket full of coppers, so it wasn't such a bad evening.

Christmas, joy to all men, and the rest of it, all

depended on one thing. Yep, that's right— whether my dad was working or not. This time of year was particularly good or particularly bad, because in the grove we used to gather in the square every year after the queen's speech at three O'clock sharp, to tell each other what we had for Christmas. The richer kids would brag about the fact that they had so many presents they had still not opened all of them by the queens speech and that they had to have a break because they were tired. 'A break because they were tired'— bastards!

After they had wiped the blood from their noses, I told them that they were very lucky and should go in immediately before they got smacked again. I, however, told them that I had received a lot more things than I actually did. If they asked to come and play with it, I would make some excuse why we couldn't. Like the dog had just died, or the door was jammed, or there was a fire at the bottom of the stairs and we were waiting for the fire brigade. Sometimes it was awful— the build-up to Christmas Day. I would make a list and look at the best presents of the day. Action Man was my favourite. Some years, when Dad was working, it was great and, one year, I got a scooter from McGauley's.

McGauley's was a toy shop just down from the chip shop on Coventry Road, just past the bus garage. This shop was my absolute dream. A real old-fashioned shop with anything in there you could imagine as a child. I loved everything about that shop. The smell of toys that were brand new, plastic and wood, and fresh new cardboard. Train sets continuously going around on displays— wonderful. An old man used to run it and he used to wear a shirt and tie and a brown coat. He was a very polite man and softly-spoken— perfect for a shopkeeper. I talked to him a lot when I used to buy my model planes there. I used to do them and hang them from my bedroom ceiling, until

Seamus started to throw his clogged shoes at them, saying that the shoes were made in Germany and that we were playing war games. They would then fall to the floor in a crumpled heap. Sometimes I would come home from school and various planes would be in a crumpled heap on my bed— mysteriously broken. Seamus, of course, had nothing to do with it, and would just sit there sniggering. So I then used to pee in his bed when he went out and said to myself that it was raining in the trenches and would obviously get wet, laughing loudly whilst peeing. He, of course, would not notice this until he got in, and by that time it was too late. He had already sat in it. I used to pee in his bed all the time. Even a few times whilst he was still in it. It was worth the smack in the mouth after I had just peed on his head whilst he was sleeping.

Anyway, back to McGauley's and this scooter. I had been looking at this scooter in the window of the shop for about a month. They had put it in the display in the window with all the bright lights, and as soon as I walked passed I double-backed and was dumbstruck. It was a big red scooter with breaks and big chunky wheels. It was just amazing. I thought, *imagine if I get that for Christmas— it would be amazing.*

Then I remembered what I got the year before, and I thought there was no chance. The year before was a torrid affair. Dad had not worked for some time, and Christmas was looming.

Not going to be good this year, I thought. And it wasn't. That year, I got an apple. A bloody apple. Seamus got an orange and so we put them together and had a fruit salad. Pathetic. Ooh, the thought of it. I could honestly say that was the worst Christmas I ever had. We didn't even have a chicken, never mind a turkey. I think we had beans on toast for Christmas dinner, and no money for electricity, TV or Brian, the milkman. Anyway, this scooter. So, I was

outside the toy shop, dribbling on the pavement. It was just
the perfect gift for me. Then I looked at the price tag:
twenty-five pounds.

Twenty-five pounds! Well, back in 1977 that was a lot
of money. A weeks wages for some folk. So I just walked
away disappointed again and told myself to forget it. It was
impossible. I told my dad about it, and he said he would
take a look, but, generally, I knew that he was just saying
that to keep me quiet. I said okay, and that was that. He
was working through November and right up until the
Christmas break, but I still never thought that I would get
it. In those days, you normally got one main present and
two or three smaller ones. Sometimes, one smaller one and
no main. So Christmas Day came, and all I could see under
the plastic tree that we pulled out of the loft every year
with the same red and gold trimmings and paper lanterns,
was one smaller present. *What the bloody hell is going on*, I
thought. Everybody else has main presents, and I just had
this. An outrage. There would be a letter in the post to
Santa Clause immediately. I didn't really believe in Santa
Clause— I was just saying that for effect. Anyway, the
complaints came thick and fast, and I wasn't really listening
to the feeble excuses. Not reasons, but excuses as to why I
got this little whatever-it-was and, frankly, didn't care,
excuse for a present. Dad just shook his head, laughed, and
left the room.

"That's it! Walk away when I'm talking. Just ignore
me!" I shouted after him.

Just then, he rolled the scooter in with a great big ribbon
on it. Well I never did and I never would. I couldn't believe
it. The very same scooter as the one I saw in McGauley's. I
don't know what I had done to deserve this. Nothing
probably, but I took it anyway. I span around the room
with it, almost knocking over the tree and getting wrapped
up in all the tinsel, which looked like flames coming out the

back of my scooter. I was Evel Knievel on a scooter. I never got off it all day, and as soon as breakfast was over I was out around the grove on it. It was so fast. I even cleaned it when I came in so it would be sparkling when I showed my friends later. I must say that it was the best Christmas present I ever got. It was superb. Not only because it was such a surprise, but I know Mom and Dad went out on a limb to get it, and that meant an awful lot then, and still does.

The one thing I do remember about all the Christmases as a child was the visits from my Uncle Eddie and Auntie Pauline, with their son, Martin. Eddie was my dad's younger brother, and was a real grafter. He was a clever man who did what he had to— a great father to Martin and a wonderful husband to Pauline. A strong admirable man with lots of qualities I wish I had now.

I have tried to live up to what Eddie might have expected of me for many years, and I hope I have done him proud. We were very close. I loved him like a father and a best friend. The relationship we had I will never have again. It was lost when he died of cancer at the age of sixty.

I was devastated. I remember visiting him in hospital many times and wondering why is this man suffering when he has brought nothing but good in his life. The tears flowed continuously during my visits to Eddie. I was a wreck. I could never hold it together and I never tried. He knew how I felt before he died, and I made sure he knew. He was a great, great man and is sorely missed. The question is, why do all the good ones die young, or younger than the people who make other people's lives a misery? I will never understand this.

However, I will always remember their visits on Christmas Eve. Every year without fail they would turn up, regardless of the weather, and bring us presents. They did the same to the other members of the family, too. It was a tradition of theirs to bring happiness to the less fortunate. Not by any means in a patronising way, but because they cared. They simply cared.

It was always a practical gift given by Eddie and Pauline: gloves or a hat and scarf, socks or underwear. They knew buying us games was worth nothing, but giving us things we actually needed, was better. I think it was because they wanted to take the pressure off mom and dad. Just so it was something they didn't have to think about.

The present I got was a truck. I loved it. I was only five at the time, but you had to be six to go to the party. As it was my birthday only a few weeks later, they agreed to let me go—hence the six years label on my jumper.

Christmas of 1971 at my granddad's factory Christmas party.

13

Granny and Granddad

THROUGHOUT MY WHOLE CHILDHOOD, AS FAR BACK AS I can remember, there were Granny and Granddad. That is, until 1974. Then they moved back to Ireland to die. They said that later anyway. They were extremely hard working people, and hardly rested a day in their lives. They were my moms parents, and very proud. My dad lost both parents by the time he was six years old. Hell of a thing to happen. Tommy, my dads older brother, looked after five younger siblings when he was just sixteen, until they were dispersed to various people. Their dad died at the age of forty-two, three years after the D-Day landings of which he had been a part. He died of TB. Their mom died at the age of just thirty-nine, also from TB. That would be a story to tell, I can tell you. Tommy was one of the funniest men I have ever met. He was also hiding from the torment of those early years. I loved him dearly. He was a truly desperate man. The story goes he used to fight drunks when they came out of the pubs for money so he could feed the kids. The welfare and the church turned their backs on him. He was alone until distant aunts took pity. Some were nice, some were not. Some were worse than the devil himself.

The family was split up, so I never knew my

grandparents on my father's side at all. I have pictures, though, and they both were very handsome. It is probably where I get my genetically rigid jaw line from. Yeah right.

So, as you can imagine, when my grandparents decided to move back to Ireland, I wasn't too pleased. From the age of about five or six, I used to go up there every Sunday morning— even if I had been up there the day before, just so I could have a slice of home made bread. My granny was a great cook and had to be with fourteen kids. Being Irish, Catholic and having a broken TV, what else could you do? My granny said my granddad only had to shake his trousers at her and she was pregnant. They only did it the fourteen times though, she swears. She was the kind of woman who could take everything in her stride and laugh at it— a strong woman who had a heart of gold. Throughout her life she had two strokes and two heart attacks, as well as a few other major illnesses. It was as though she was asking God if that was the best he could do to see her off. She was a tough old broad and I loved her. She passed away in her sleep at the age of eighty-four. She ran the household like an army and had to. She used to get up early, bake the bread, cook all the breakfast for all the kids and Granddad, and then do a full-time job. After work, she got back home to cook all the dinners, ready for when everybody came home.

She, as every Irish woman, had a dowry when she married. She brought it with her— a mixture of furnishings, porcelain and cutlery, money and jewellery, which was passed down from her mom and her moms mom. This dowry was under lock and key in the parlour room. Granddad never set foot in there as long as I remember. He wasn't allowed to. Only the priest and I went in that room. It was the finest room I had ever seen. I was there one day helping Granny with the cleaning, and she said that I had better hurry up a bit, as the priest was coming to visit, and she was going to entertain him in the parlour. I asked whether she was going to play the banjo or sing a song. She said no and laughed. She said that she was only going to have tea and biscuits. *That's great*, I thought. I headed towards the downstairs toilet and the carbolic soap. That I wasn't too happy over, but the priest was coming, so it had to be done.

The priest turned up late, and didn't even apologise, the ignorant git. My granny told him so too, but he said nothing. I know this got to my granny, because she never got her best biscuits out. I laughed because I knew he was eating the cheap ones, but he was happy anyway. Well, they talked about boring stuff and the church and rubbish like that, which, for a six- or seven-year-old, was not exciting at all. After a while, he said he had to go and that God's work was calling, and that it was never done. I just sat there looking around the room, looking at all the sparkly stuff. Then she saw the priest out, and came and coaxed me out of the parlour. The door was locked and the key put in her apron pocket.

"Don't tell anybody about the dowry now," she said, "or the dogs will have the lot away."

I said I wouldn't. She collected the tea tray, and we went back into the kitchen to clean up. She gave me a big slice of cake and sat and told stories until my mom came to fetch me. She was just lovely and doted on the kids.

Anyway, the bread. I used to go up and have a slice of bread, knowing full well she would ask me if I wanted to have some breakfast, too. Of course, it would have been rude to refuse. So I didn't. I lapped the lot up quicker than quick. Absolutely delicious. Then I would mess around with Granddad for a while. He never said much, but I liked him. All the other grandkids were frightened to death of him, but I used to play him up. He was a short man, but as wide as the door. He came from Dublin and was a painter.

Not a constable-type painter: you know— landscapes. He was a painter of houses. He had been a builder before his accident. He had fallen off a church steeple and broken both his legs and his arm. He said thank God he never landed on his thing. With fourteen kids, you would think that he had had enough, wouldn't you? He had shoulders on him like a horse. My lasting image of my granddad was him sitting in his chair and reading his paper. He would occasionally look over the top, suck on his pipe, and go back to his reading.

After winding up Granddad, I would say my goodbyes, and then trot on home. I saw them a lot before they went back to Ireland. Granny used to work at Wimbush bakery, just off Green Lane by the baths. Every time I went swimming— which was often in the summer holidays and in the winter with school— I would pop in and say hello. She would give me a load of iced buns and I would eat them in the library, if it was open, or would go home and eat the lot before I got in and the hyenas pounced.

I used to go up on Saturday mornings in the early days, and the other cousins would meet us there. Apparently, Rory, my Uncle Rory's son, used to punch me straight in the mouth every time I had my back turned. My granddad told Rory senior, and he would tell him off. I just let it go; I was biding my time. This happened about three times until, one day, he tried the same thing again and I knocked his lights out. My granddad was amazed at how quick I was and how many times I hit him. He said I was like lightning and I hit him about six or seven times in about two seconds. He was so proud of me, and he wasn't fond of Rory, because he was a bit of a bully. He never hit anyone else after that day. I think that's why Granddad had a soft spot for me— because I wouldn't back down. He knew that I would be okay.

My granddad worked in a factory most of his working life— a far cry from the fields of Ireland. He knew, though, that he had to earn the money for the family, and I'm not sure if he enjoyed it, but he had to do it anyway. Well, that's what you get for 'fourteen times thirty' seconds of passion.

14

Wimbush Bakery, Green Lane Swimming and the Library

As STATED PREVIOUSLY, GRANNY WORKED AT the cake factory. Ummm! I used to go there after swimming when I was starving hungry. Swimming is something I did as a kid. Green Lane swimming baths was brilliant. It was an old Victorian building, again fantastic architecture.

It was also very good when the council closed it. I was in that place for about six weeks stripping it of copper and lead and whatever precious metals I could get hold of. The roof was full of lead and that took a bit of time, mainly because it was so high. Maybe ten to twelve metres high. I dropped the lead off and it hit the floor hard. I had to drop it when something heavy passed on the road and drop it into the baths' courtyard. I then hid it in the grounds, away from prying eyes. I went back to get it one day, and the whole lot had gone. Everything. They must have had a truck in there to take the lot away. I went down to see my man at the scrap yard, and he said he hadn't had a delivery of that description in at all. If he did, he would let me know. I didn't hear anything, so that was that. Thieving bastards; you can't trust anybody, can you?

I used to go in to the baths and immediately smell the chlorine. It hit me like a misplaced shoe. You then paid the money and you would get a box with an elastic, coloured band with a number on it. You would then get changed at the side of the pool in a cubicle. The box would be then taken back and given to the person behind the counter. Then you were free. I always used to dive in the deep end and just go for it. I was not a bad swimmer, but not Tarzan neither.

The door to the baths was on the right forked road, about fifty metres past the bus stop. Wimbush bakery was on the left fork; it was the opposite building. The pub where Uncle Y took me was just past Wimbush, on the same side as the library. Graceful.

Mark Smith was like Johnny Weissmuller from Tarzan, but me more like the monkey. It was great fun all the same. I used to take in a copper or two, throw it in the pool and dive down and get it. When I went with Seamus, he would dive down as well and hold me down under the water until I swallowed a good chunk of the pool. I hated him.

One day he pushed me too far and was winding me up on the side of the pool. I just jumped in the air and landed with two feet straight in his cock-eyed face. He went under, and I didn't say a word to the lifesaver. He was then spotted by another and rescued. He came to, punched me in the mouth, and was thrown out for violence. It was a good day, and worth the thick lip. I had a great day with my mates, and it lasted for hours and hours.

At the end of every session, I would collect my clothes and get dressed in the cubicle and give the box back with the band. I would then collect my cakes from Granny, and, if I didn't go straight home, I would go into the library. The library was attached to the swimming baths in the same Victorian building. It was a fantastic old library, which I loved being in— then and still today. I love the smell of old books. The way they feel and, of course, the knowledge gained and education received from beneath the covers, astounds me. I would sit for hours and just look through the great works. And although I could not understand them at that time, I appreciated their value. To be a part of an establishment even though I was not a scholar, and am still not, was warming to me. I could sit and not be judged, as I was just another kid in the library. I would be left amongst the shadows and blend in nicely. It was comforting.

I met friends there and we read books together. Reading was something I enjoyed immensely and would to use escape to far off worlds in *Gulliver's Travels* and *Robinson Crusoe*. I would be lost until the sun went down. In the summer, the library would be open until 8 p.m., and it became my second home. What the hell did I want to go home for? I had no idea what would be waiting for me. Dad drinking? No food? Constant bullying? Maybe even no electricity or TV.

No thanks. I will stay where I was until I was thrown out— which was often. I would be filled with dread going home. Walking past the police station and past McGauley's, and then past the bus station. By the time I was two hundred metres from home, I would have a knot in my stomach as big as a football. It was horrible. Climbing the back fence and in the door and up the stairs.

"Hiya, Ginge!" *Smack.*

Seamus was so kind. Welcome home Christian, welcome home.

I spent many happy days in the library, and would often talk to old people. I loved listening to their stories— hypnotised, I would listen for hours to their adventures, and what they did and where. Some fought in the war and lived to tell the tale. How they were drafted into the army at seventeen to go fight in faraway lands against an enemy they hadn't known much about and, very often, hadn't even seen until they were on top of them. And the reason they were given for risking their life was 'their country'— the very country that failed them every day when they retired with their penny pinching.

"Was it really all worth it?" I used to ask them.

They would say, "Yes, it was."

"There is always the possibility of change, because we live in a democratic state," they would say. "Under Hitler, we would never have been so fortunate. We were not just fighting for our lives— we were fighting for the lives of our children and our children's children. How could we lose? Losing was not an option."

The words were said with such emotion that I realised that they lived with the horrors and memories of war every day.

Others did lose. Others were not so fortunate to see the rewards of victory. I wondered how it would be at the age of seventeen to be killed in a faraway land and your relatives and loved ones not being able to grieve at your graveside. In some instances not even find your body and literally be in No Man's Land.

I often used to meet a neighbour of mine, Mr.Coventry. He was the gentlest man and I would often run errands for him. A packet of Old Holborn tobacco and a packet of Swan Vesta matches. He used to give me the money and off I would go on my go-cart and be back in no time. He used to give me a few coppers for going. Mr.Coventry would often come into the library when I was there, and we would sit together. It was like having my granddad back again. He used to teach me a lot, when in the library, about looking for certain books and what reference to use. Then he would sit and read his books and I would read mine. He would often leave a little earlier than me, as he didn't like to be out late. Strange, isn't it? A man like Mr. Coventry who fought in the war, did his bit for king and country, and he didn't like to be out late. An outrage, that's what it was. The same things happen today. Whatever happened to respect? Whatever colour or creed, everybody deserves respect for what they are and what or in whom they believe in. Why is there prejudice in the world? From the darkest streets to the open plains.

Mr.Coventry moved from Pleasant Park a few years later over to the new estate. I visited him a few times, but he wasn't happy. He said that some of the kids were making it difficult for him. I knew who they were, and told them to stop, or else. I told them he was my granddad and that there would be war if they didn't. They stopped, and the friends I had made sure it didn't continue. He settled down a bit, but I think he was even more frightened there than in Pleasant Park. It was a lot bigger and there were more people. My friends, Carlton and Davindar, lived close, and I asked them to keep an eye out for him.

He didn't come to the library much more, either, so I was losing yet another one of the family— another Granddad. The library seemed to lose its appeal for a while and I didn't go much, either. I just closed up for a bit. Looking back this was a sad stage in my life— again. I wasn't reading as much, school was not as good for some reason or another, and Dad was drinking again. It always seemed like there was something going on that was determined to make my life miserable. I remember very clearly, at this stage, sitting on my bedroom windowsill one evening when Seamus was away and looking out over the railway track. Life was so much better over that side, and I was thinking about my life and wondering, *what the bloody hell am I doing here? What is the meaning of my life?* I thought there must be something big waiting for me later on, as I wasn't the kind to throw in the towel. I had thought about suicide, but not seriously. I had thought that I didn't want to live this way anymore, but what could I do? I was trapped in a spiral heading down, and the only way up was to fight. So that is exactly what I did. I fought and made my way out of the depression I was in. I'm not sure why it wasn't noticed at school. I think I just put a brave face on. I do not blame the teachers in any way, shape or form— it was just the way it was.

I eventually found my way back into the library and accepted my life for what it was. I think it made me stronger. I enjoyed the books. I just got my head down and read book after book, waiting for the sun to come out again, which it did.

15

Birmingham City Football Club

Since I lived only a stone's throw from the BCFC, it was very difficult not to get wrapped up in the place. When you live so close, the atmosphere closes around you, and it's fantastic. When the season began in late August, the tension was electric. There was much anticipation regarding the summer signings, and maybe this will be the year the Blues get through to the FA Cup final and finally take the cup home and slot it into the trophy cabinet. For those of you who are not familiar with English football, the FA Cup is the most prestigious cup in English football. The Blue Boys, or the 'Blues', as Birmingham City are fondly known, did not hold the trophy often. During the war, the playing field was hit twenty times, and they didn't start playing there until 1943. The players even had to change in a nearby factory.

During the seventies when I was a child, players came and went, but one will always remain the people's favourite: Trevor Francis. What a player he was. He was quick and skilful and a brilliant all-round player. He played two hundred and seventy-eight games for the Blues and scored one hundred and twenty-eight goals. Fantastic.

He was most certainly my hero at that time. During

every match game, because we were so close to the ground, there was certainly room for scams. The posh people used to bring their cars up the grove and we would look after it for them. As soon as they arrived, I was out. Sometimes I would be right at the end of the street, telling them there was a parking place free and I would then look after their car whilst they were enjoying the game. It wasn't very often that anything happened, but, when it did, we took the registration number if there was a bump, and would give it to the driver when he returned. For this service, we would charge a fee. It was the driver's discretion as to how much we would get, but most of the time it was ten or twenty pence. On rare occasions, it was more. I got two pounds, once, for looking after a Jaguar Mark II. It was a fantastic car, and I sat out there the whole time watching it. All the other kids gathered around and admired the quality. We were thugs, but we were cultured thugs. Most days, I would listen to opera on Radio Two. I didn't tell the other kids that, of course. When asked about the racket on the radio, I would say it was my dad listening to it. However, it was really me. I loved it, and still do.

Yes, the Jaguar. So anyway, I looked after it, and the Blues were winning. Although the game wasn't finished yet, the owner had returned and was obviously very happy. He said he knew the score when it came to this sort of caper, the minding of cars. I told him I hadn't moved a centimetre and he could ask my dad if he wanted. He said it wasn't necessary, as he believed me. He reached into his pocket and pulled out two pound notes. Usually, when they do that, they move the folding stuff to one side and look for the pennies. Not this guy, though— he gave me two pound notes and said, "Remember this, son. If you work for a living, you will get good money."

I said I would remember it, and told him to come back next home game, and I'd look after it again. I was delighted.

The next home game came and I took some police cones that the traffic police had put up further down the road, to stop people parking on corners and stuff, and placed them just outside my house. I waited for the Jaguar to come back, but he didn't come. He obviously got a parking place somewhere else. I bet he didn't get the same service, though.

I watched a lot of football at the Blues club in those days. I was there when George Best played for Fulham— I think it was 1974 to 1975. He was playing alongside Rodney Marsh, another fantastic player. They tore the Blues apart. Rodney Marsh was outstanding and some people said that George Best was a genius. He was an entertainer. He wowed the fans with his style of play, and he could grab all fifty thousand fans' attention and play with your emotions like a magician. He hypnotised you with his play, and didn't let you go until he was ready. He was a wonderful player, and I, as a lad, had the pleasure of watching him play. I will never forget it, and the fact that he was an Irishman was just a bonus.

I didn't pay in, of course. If I wanted to watch the whole game, I would often sneak in with Thomas Maloney or Chris O'Hara over the fence. Most of the lads from the grove went to the game. It was part and parcel of growing up. My dad never went, because he was scared stiff of the crowds. He said it felt like the crowds were trying to squeeze the life out of him. So I went with the boys. In those days they let the gates open at half time and you could walk in for free. It was brilliant. I would then go and see Francis, my cousin remember, who was working as a pie salesman at the ground. For years he gave me free pies. Anything I wanted— sometimes he gave me a pocket full of cash from pies he had sold and pocketed the money. He had sewn a second pocket in the lining of his trousers so he could pocket the coins without anyone knowing. If anyone gave him the folding stuff, he would just put that down his sock when no one was looking. He was a master criminal and it showed. The games would just fly by when you had a steak and kidney pie and a cup of Bovril. Bovril was a hot beef extract drink and was very tasty. Just the kind of thing you needed when stuck on a football terrace in winter, I can tell you. Francis used to work on the reserve matches as well, but the money wasn't as good. I used to get in for free, as he got me a job as ball boy. The ball boy's job was to retrieve the ball when the players kicked it out. If you got the Spion Kop end, you got the short straw. This was one of the biggest terraced stands in the whole club and it was murder running up and down when the ball was kicked into the back of the stand. I did it anyway, because you could get close to the players and get lots of autographs.

During the seventies, when the football was in full swing, there was also an element of football fans that let their frustrations out. This type of fan was commonly known as the 'football hooligan'. There a lot of these in English football, and I was a victim more than once. I remember actually standing in the away end, which was the Tilton end. All the away fans got a smaller stand and all the home fans got the bigger stand. I would say the home fans outnumbered the away fans by six to one. I was supporting Manchester United and was with Sylvester and Cyril, my singing partners. The Manchester fans had been given the small stand and packed it to the rafters. They were perhaps about three thousand. Manchester was in fine form and with ten minutes to go, were leading four to one. There was no hope for the Blues and people started to disappear. All the fans vanished and I was a bit worried, to say the least. I knew it meant only one thing: the Blues fans were going to relieve some frustration and have a good old punch up. It was normal, in those days, for the police to escort all the away fans from the ground, through to New Street train station in the city centre, for the ride home. Which, I suppose, was about two kilometres. The police on horseback would stop any fans who came forward, but when bottles were thrown, the police had no chance.

So the final whistle had gone, and the away fans were now to be let out of the away end and escorted to potential safety. Outside were about two hundred police officers, with about twenty on horseback. They were about seven metres apart, and in two lines on both sides of the fence. At the other end of this funnel were eleven thousand Blues fans. It looked like it was going to end in tears, so I just bolted straight through the line of policemen and headed across some waste ground and over a wall attached to the school. All hell broke loose. People were getting slashed with knives and bottles. Bricks were thrown and bouncing off people's heads. It was madness. The police, trying to keep the peace, were right in the thick of it. They were getting hammered and, for five or so minutes, I honestly thought that I had got away with it. I hadn't. I got spotted by a group of skinheads. I bolted through the playground and, since I knew the school well, as I used it often, I thought, *I know just where to go*. There was a second-level playground, and, to reach it, you would go up a set of steps. At the top was a gate that was never locked... up till that day. I ran up the steps to the top, and tried the gate.

It was locked. The skinheads had already reached the bottom step, and were making their way up slowly and methodically. As the steps were enclosed by a wire mesh, there was nowhere for me to go. So I just got ready for the biggest smacking of my life. I must say that, when you resign yourself to such a thing, you know it's going to happen, so you just go with the flow. You are scared, of course, but you just accept the fact that you are going to get a kicking. I tried to tell them that I was a local lad, but they wouldn't listen. I got a few punches in, but that only made it worse. I remember curling up in the corner by the gate, and that was that. I woke up a while later, and knew that I had indeed, had a good kicking. My eyebrow was split wide open where I think I got booted in the face. My nose was broken, and my lip was swollen. My ribs were aching, and the tops of my legs were heavily bruised. I had obviously passed out, but had no idea for how long. It took me a while to get home, and, when I did finally walk through the door, no one was home. For the first time in my life, I could really have done with some tender loving care, but no— the same as usual. *Look after yourself, Christian; no one else will.* I went straight up the stairs— which was agony— and into the bathroom. I looked at myself in the mirror and thought I had been in a train wreck. I washed my face and that hurt like hell, and dabbed the towel to my face to dry off. I went to bed and pulled my bed clothes over my body. It was a rough night's sleep, and, when Seamus tried to wake me up in the usual fashion, he stopped. He actually thought I was dead and called Mom. She came and sat me down. Some of the swelling had gone down, but the eye was twice the size. It was the worst I had ever been and it took me a week to get over it. And to think, this beating was from my own team supporters— great, eh. Mom really looked after me, and Dad said that I wouldn't be able to go to football matches again. Of course, I did. I was just careful about where I stood.

16

Canals and Aquaducts

AROUND THE CITY CENTRE AND WHERE I LIVED WAS a network of canals and aqueducts. Of course, being a young boy, these were fascinating places. In the summer, I used to walk the canal paths and help the barges go through the locks. The science of it intrigued me. I also used to jump aboard the barges and chat to the people on it. I would travel a few kilometres, and then jump on another, which would then take me back to the same place. The traffic was quite heavy in the summer, and it was never any problem getting lifts.

We used to play 'skimming'. That means we used to get flat stones and skim them across the water. The stone would skip across the water and the one with the most hits on the surface of the water, won. It was a simple game, but we would play this for hours. Of course, we were aware of the dangers playing near the canal side, but we didn't take it very seriously. I didn't look at danger the same way. You don't as a child. You are invincible. Take climbing trees, for instance. I do not know a man in the land who didn't climb trees. There used to be a big oak tree close to where we lived. It was maybe twenty metres high. During one tree-climbing session, a few of the gang climbed to the top— almost all the way. It's a long way down, but we were never afraid. It was just a game. The first one to the top wins. No matter how high. The canals were the same. We used to play around the locks and dare each other to jump from one side of the canal to the other. Kevin was a good jumper and made it without any problem, every time. I had a bit of trouble now and again, and would hit the side and drag myself out, or leave a trailing foot that would be wet for a few hours. Playing near the canal was good fun until, that is, we had the fright of our lives.

Running parallel to the canal were overflow systems that would drain into a big reservoir on the other side of town. There were a lot of us and we decided to track it down and try and gain access and see where it led to. Eventually we climbed down a ladder and into the overflow system. The walls were about four metres high and there were tunnels coming from everywhere. We decided to follow the flow of water that was only a trickle and see where it went. We were to find out later that this was the main inlet. All the water that overflowed in this area, not only from the canal, but also the drains and gulleys in the streets, would come into the main inlet at this point. We walked for about an hour down this waterway and were just about getting bored when it started to rain. We didn't take much notice, as it was only a light shower. It was more of an inconvenience that we might get a little wet than anything else. Until, that is, the water level started to rise slightly. Before that, we could walk quite nicely at the sides of the flowing water. Now the water was lapping at our feet in places. I was wondering what was going on, and thought that maybe the canal had narrowed slightly. It had not narrowed— it had widened, and it was still lapping at our feet. We were in trouble. The rain became heavier and heavier as we made our way, now quicker, down the channel. The water was suddenly flowing quicker, and was now at our knees as we waded in it, looking for a way out.

There was a smaller tunnel ahead, which was probably another outlet to drain the main channel. I had no idea where it went, but I could see the other end. I don't know why I did it, but I took control. There were guys much older than me and, usually, the oldest would always take charge in emergencies. Or what we classed as emergencies. Not this time. I told them that we should take the smaller tunnel, since there was a possibility that this was draining the access water from the main channel. Strangely everyone agreed and down we went. It was smaller and you could stretch out and touch both sides. I was crouching almost all the way down, but just kept going all the same. The others followed. I was at the front and leading them to safety— or thought I was. We kept going until we came to the end, the water rising all the time. To our left, we could see the main channel again, and it was probably three metres high by now. So I think we made the right decision there. We rested a while. Then someone else noticed that there was a ladder to our right, about twelve metres away. We grabbed our chance and scrambled up to the roadside. We were safe. Some of the older boys tapped me on the back and said, "Good job."

I was pleased, but it was that day that has stayed with me.

The canal's sides were also good for scams, since in the olden days, as you are probably aware, they used to use the canals as trade runs. All the trade passed through the canals and all the deliveries were hoisted up and into the factories and shops. A lot of the shops therefore still had their premises backing on to the canal tow paths. I utilised this as much as I could. I will tell you of one instance. There was a very well-known bicycle shop where I used to collect the usual things for bicycle repairs. I used to fix everything myself with bicycles in those days. I could strip a bike down and have it working again by the end of the day—

bearings re-greased and ready for another bashing. This particular bicycle shop was the nearest to home, and had good stock. It worked for me. I used to go in and see all the latest models, and drool over the paintwork and such, but would only buy a puncture repair kit for the seventy-forth time. I never spent over twenty pence. What a customer, eh.

Anyway, the bikes were fantastic. I, however, had my brother's foldaway ladies' bicycle that had also been my sister's at one point. The thing had travelled around the globe. It had more kilometres on it than a London cab. Dad, however, refused to part with it until it was absolutely destroyed— knowing full well it would outlive him. The Raleigh Chopper was out of my league— so was the newer model— and was to be an outstanding all-terrain bicycle. The Raleigh Grifter, this was a special bike. It was tough and durable. Scale anything with its three-speeds hand-grip changer, and it looked dynamite. This was the ultimate in pedal pushing. I would never have one. The foldaway would stay with me until I destroyed it or it destroyed me.

The canal tow path was my only chance at getting one, I thought, and, since I dreamt of riding the Grifter with the wind in my afro, I had to get a plan. I did get a plan. It was this: at night, I would make my way into the back of the shop, obtain a Grifter, and tell my dad that it was a friend's and I was looking after it for him. All the contraband that entered the house this way followed the same road. I was looking after it for someone. So one, evening, I did exactly that. I collected my tools, and had my 'milk tray advert' clothes on, all black— evening wear for burglars and wannabe romancers— and headed out on my go-cart, down the hill and onto the tow path. No one had seen me, so phase one was completed. Check.

I sat around on my cart for a few minutes, waiting for the police to feel my collar. Nothing. After hiding my cart, I climbed over the fence and into the backyard. Phase two completed. Check.

Why do I keep saying check? I didn't have it written down; I just kept saying it. I was the six million dollar man. Every time I did anything that required speed or strength, I hummed the tune. Get back to the story, Christian, for Christ's sake.

Okay. I was over the fence and squaring up the back door. *Well, well, well. What do we have here then?* I took my torch out of my satchel. It looked like a Yale lock. *A double cylinder and strengthened*, I said to myself in the only safe cracking voice I knew. It's not that I could deduce a lock's strength or capacity just by looking at it. It's what it said on the lock. I had absolutely no chance of breaking that, I thought. Not with tatting tools, anyway. So I just left it at that. I was resigned to giving up. Then, out the corner of my eye, there stood a bicycle. Would you believe it? It looks far better than mine. It is a bit racy, so it will do for a night's work. I climbed to the top of the fence again to make sure no one was around. I jumped down and grabbed the bike. I managed to climb to the top of the fence again whilst holding the bike with one hand. I hoisted the front wheel and hooked it on at the top of the fence. I then jumped down and hoisted the seat over one of the posts. The bike was just hanging there. I climbed to the top again and pushed the bike over the top and held it swinging for a while until I let it go and it hit the ground with a bang. I ducked down below the fence for a few seconds, and then looked again to make sure no one had heard the crime of the century in progress.

I scaled the fence and dropped to the floor. The bike wasn't mine yet. I still had to get it home.

I couldn't take both at the same time. I had to come back for one. The go-cart was my life's blood. I couldn't leave that, so I jumped on it and took it home. I then returned for the bike. Travelling without lights, as you know, was guaranteed to attract attention, so I brought lights with me. I didn't have time to fix them properly, so I just tied them on with a bit of string. Off I went and, within no time, I was bouncing up the steps to the flat. On the way home, I realised, though, that I couldn't pedal backwards, and thought that it was probably jammed. So I didn't think more about it and pushed up against the back of the cart for support and to keep it from falling over. This would be a job for me in the morning, I thought, and was very happy with my night's work. I slept soundly and bounded down the stairs early morning to take a closer look at my prize. It wasn't as good as I thought. It wasn't anywhere close to good. The bike itself was about fifty years old and had a fixed wheel. This meant that it was only used for the track— time trials. It would be useless for the streets. It also had solid rubber tyres, so if you went over even the smallest pebble it would vibrate your teeth out. It was not the best scam I ever did, but you have to try, don't you? In truth, it was disaster.

17

In-Laws and Outlaws

MY DAD'S SIBLINGS WERE TOMMY, HUGH, JOE, EDDIE and Helen. Eddie, Tommy, and Helen I have mentioned earlier. Joe died when I was eleven, I think, around 1976 to 1977. He was a roofer and one of the hazards of the job was falling, and that's exactly what he did. He fell off the roof and died. He was forty-two. Hugh left the Belfast shipyard when he was fifteen and never looked back. He ended up in Canada working as a merchant sea captain and retired there. He still lives in Canada and growing up he was this exotic sea captain that not many people knew about. He came back to England occasionally and spent some time with the outlaws and then went home again. He was an enigma. He brought his family over a few times. He was great.

Speaking of Canada, we had a neighbour called Mrs. Grover. She lived directly next door on the first floor. She was a big woman and found it difficult to get around. So Mom used to help her around the house and fetch her some groceries, make tea, things like that. Anyway, she died after a long illness. Her son, who was evacuated to Canada in the war when he was four or five, came over with his wife and sorted out all the arrangements for the funeral. He knew of my mother's help towards his mother, and thanked her. They were invited to our place for tea and sandwiches.

They came and were very nice. I didn't pay too much attention to the conversation.

Apparently, it went something like this: the couple were not able to have children, and wondered if they could take me back to Canada with them. If I liked it there, and they thought it was working, they would ask my parents if they could adopt me. They would organise everything on that side and it was up to my parents as to allow the experiment to happen. I didn't realise what was going on, but apparently my dad said no way, and that he could bring up his own kids. That was the end of that. I wonder what my life would have been like if they had said yes.

Apart from Uncle Y, I had many more uncles and aunts. Uncle Paddy was a real joker, and liked a tipple. One day he came around to our place and was asked if he would like to stay for dinner. He said he would love to, as he was starving hungry. An hour later dinner was served and I remember exactly what it was: sausage and mashed potatoes. I used to up-end the sausages and stick them in the top of the mash like horns. I did this every time.

There was a knock at the door. It was my pal and I told him I was eating my dinner and would be out again soon. I then returned to the table in a bit of a hurry to get out, so I started eating the dinner quickly— not paying too much attention to the dinner itself. I was nearly at the bottom of the mash when *clunk*. I had bitten into something hard. I pulled out the object and then realised that it was teeth. Uncle Paddy had put his false teeth at the bottom of my mash for me to find.

He was a heavy smoker and, as I said, he liked a tipple. The teeth were all brown and filthy and needed a clean. They were in such a state that sulphuric acid would probably have been the only thing that could clean them. I couldn't believe it. I screamed, and Paddy and the rest of the family just rolled around laughing. Paddy took the teeth back, licked off the remaining potato and slotted them back in his mouth. I, meanwhile, was off like a shot to clean my teeth thoroughly.

Another uncle was Jimmy. He was a good looking lad only 13 years older than me and brilliant at football. He could have been a professional, but found girls and beer, and that was the end of that budding career. I liked Jimmy. He had a real zest for life back then and still does. I wonder how his life would have been if only he would have gone the other way.

Aunty Patty was different. When she got bored, she used to ask my mom if I could stay at her place, which was two bus rides away. I hated it. She was a nice woman, but it was really boring. There was no television and the furniture was sparse, to say the least. She didn't have much money, so it was a tough time for her. I went because I felt sorry for her. The problem was that I would have to stay there for long periods— sometimes two or three weeks. And I would have to sleep on the floor because I wet the bed. She had boyfriends and, of course, they would stay over and stuff. In a small apartment, the sound would travel, and that would be really embarrassing. One particular boyfriend was an evil bastard. He beat her up and almost killed her. I was there at the time and tried to get him off her, but he just pushed me away. I was scared stiff and just cowered in the corner. He just kept hitting her. Eventually he stopped and he walked out the door. I went and knocked on a neighbour's door, and they came running to help. They called the ambulance and whilst we were waiting for them to arrive, she died. I was crying. Then the ambulance crew ran in and took over. They brought her back to life. Afterwards she told me that she had had an out of body experience and that she actually came out of her body and saw the emergency crew working on her. Then there was a big jolt and she was back in her body. She was never the same after that and after many years fighting depression, she fell to her death from a tower block window on the ninth floor. Ironically, it was only metres away from Dixon Road School, where I spent so many happy days as a child. I recently went back there researching this book, and saw the actual place where she landed. Horrific.

Another aunt was Mora. I remember her coming down often with her husband, Bob, and three kids: Bobby, the eldest, Tony and Aemon. We got on well and played all the time. Until one day we heard that Mora was sick and that she was confined to her bed. We didn't think much of it until we got word after a few weeks that she was still sick and now had TB. I didn't really know what that was then, but I knew that it was bad. Mom went up often to see how she was, but she deteriorated quickly. She died at the age of forty-one. Bobby was seventeen and the younger kids were ten and eleven. A few years later, big Bob Moran— the kid's dad and Mora's husband— died of a massive heart attack. Bobby was just nineteen, and took both kids on. He looked after them until they were grown— a fantastic thing to do at that age. Such responsibility for a young kid.

Uncle Johnny was a bit special. Even when growing up in Pleasant park, he never came to visit. He had special needs. In those days it was either a mental home or you just got on with it. My granny and granddad, knowing them now, decided to have Johnny at home.

This wasn't without its pitfalls, mind you. He had a slight touch of Tourette's Syndrome. Well, it was more than a touch, actually. When I used to visit in the early days, I would to go in and say hello to everybody, as is customary when entering a premises, and I would, of course, say hello to Johnny, too. In return, he would tell me to fuck off. I had no idea what I had done wrong, but I asked my granny, and she said, "Just ignore him. He is in a mood again."

My granny not realising, of course, that Johnny couldn't help it. *What a great excuse*, I thought, *to go around swearing whenever you want and wherever you want, and then put it down to Tourette's.*

I looked it up in the library and wondered if it was a virus or something, but, of course, it wasn't. After spending the whole weekend with Johnny, Granny and Granddad, I did say that I had caught something off him, and I walked around swearing at everybody for a few days. Until, that is, my mom cracked, and threw me in the bathroom and washed my mouth out with carbolic soap. I didn't have Tourette's anymore. On windy days, I can still taste it.

Johnny, however, lived blissfully in his cocoon, and didn't trouble anyone really. Apart from my granny when the priest came. That was good fun, because my granny was always trying to get rid of Johnny before the priest arrived. If that didn't happen, there were fireworks. I could imagine the scene, although I was never there.

"Would you like a piece of cake, Father?" Granny asked.

"Ah, that would be grand"

"How about you Johnny?"

"F... F... Fuckoff you! Okay then."

Going straight to Hell, that man.

A few years ago, Uncle Johnny reached his sixtieth birthday.

"A living miracle," my granny said.

The doctors said he wouldn't get past thirty.

"Double the trouble," she said.

Johnny had lived with Granny and Granddad all these years, and had never had a lady friend of any kind. It was a shame, really, because he knew what parts went where— he told us often enough.

So for his sixtieth, for the crack and as a big surprise, they all chipped in and bought him a sex doll. They also dressed the doll up in stockings and suspenders, the whole works. It wasn't cheap, mind you. It was probably the most expensive realistic doll on the market. It even had real hair.

Anyway, his party was a grand affair. They had rented the local community centre and people had come from far and wide to honour this great man. They even came from abroad and a lot of planning went into it. The night came and everyone was excited, including Johnny. In the end, there was a crowd of a couple of hundred, and about half an hour into the party the ball was rolling. They took him on stage and the announcer, I think it was Paddy, said that it was great being there and so on, that people had travelled a long way to see Johnny, and he told a few jokes to get an atmosphere. Johnny, meanwhile, was getting frustrated by all this and took the mike and said that he was pleased that they were there, but to get fucking on with it because he wanted his presents. The crowd, of course, was laughing away, and then someone brought the presents on stage. Big mistake. The presents were given and told who they were from, and Johnny said, "Thanks, I will give the toaster to my Granny, bastards!"

Then, finally, out came the box with the sex doll. It was all wrapped up with very smart paper, and Paddy took his time with this one. Paddy said that all the brothers and sisters had invested a bit of money in this one and expected Johnny to really like it. He went on for a bit, and Johnny got fed up.

"Oh, fuck this!" he shouted; no mike needed there. "Just give me the fucking thing!"

The whole place was rolling and when they saw the sex doll, well, that was it. The place exploded. Johnny, meanwhile, was asked what he thought of it. He said she was beautiful. Johnny was in love. He grabbed the mike and said, "Thanks for coming, everybody, but I've got to go."

He threw the doll under his arm and went home.

Apparently he was in the bedroom for three days and only came out to go to the toilet and to go to the shed for a few supplies. My granny just gave him toast, which she slid under the door. She said that she found it so funny that she just let him get on with it.

When he came out of the bedroom eventually, the first thing he did was ask, "Is there a guarantee with this doll?"

The doll was hanging off the bed, and looked like it had been attacked by a pack of wolves. It was a bit worse for wear, to say the least. The lingerie had disappeared, and the whole thing was covered in duct tape. He had obviously got a bit carried away and had punctured it a few times. The real hair had worn away, the wig was totally misplaced, and all the colour had been scratched off with his George Michael stubble.

Who said romance was dead?

God knows how he had got on after that, but I know he never had a real girlfriend. Thank God. Yes, he was going straight to Hell.

18

Way Out West— Well, South, Actually

WELL, THE TIME IN PLEASANT PARK HAD ALMOST COME to an end. Some of my old friends have moved away and, although they had been replaced with other families and kids, it wasn't the same. The old days had gone and could never be replaced. The older lads had grown up and were doing other things, and the newer lads were not really into football. Yes, things were changing and to be honest, I wondered what I was going to do. I had moved from Dixon Road and was in the new building. It was called Regents Park now, and the Dixon Road School I knew, was dying. It was reduced to an annexe and used only occasionally. I used to look over at it when I was in the playground and realised that times must change. I had learnt, laughed and cried, met wonderful people and lost wonderful people in that building. I had kissed girls and chased them around the playground. I had fallen in love and out of love just as quickly. As long as this building stands I can come back to it and retrace the steps of long ago, happy days. It was a sad day for me when I left that school for good. It was nice going into a brand new building, but Dixon Road held a history and, more importantly, *my* history and every other child's who roamed its corridors and played in the yard. A place of education that I'm sure was as warm and as welcoming on my first day, as it was to the pupils on the first day of opening way back in the Victorian era.

My mom and dad had sat us all down just after the Christmas of 1978. Seamus wasn't there very often, and that was a blessing. Martha was going out with a guy called Kevin Shaunessy. Some good looking paddy from somewhere near the airport. That was the one day we were all at home and they had something to say. They said they had been looking at a place over in Billesley. I had never heard of it. They said it was by the country and that they had accepted it from the council. I had mixed feelings, really. Starting again might be good for me. I hadn't exactly had the best time in Pleasant Park, but it was all I knew. I had vowed never again to fight as much as I had and that I was pretty much sick of petty crime and so on. In truth I never wanted to do it in the first place, but felt I had to. So, a new beginning, eh? What could I possibly have to lose? Dad also said that he was going to clean up his act and kick the sleeping pill habit. That was good to hear. The drinking couldn't be half as bad as tablets, right?

It all sounded like good news anyway, so we all agreed that it was a good move. They said they were planning on collecting the keys form the council and we would all go over and take a look. In February 1979, we went out and had a look. It was like the country. I have never seen so many fields. It was brilliant— we could play football whenever we wanted. We looked around the area first and when we finally walked down the street to the house, I felt at home. It was a three-bedroom terrace house with two lounges. I immediately remembered my Granny's parlour room and was amazed at how big it was. Of course, when you move from a flat to a house, the size difference is vast. The one thing that I did like, though, was that we had our own garden. Yes, it was overgrown, but we would soon

knock it into shape. We had a further look around, and
Mom and Dad seemed happy. I hadn't seen them look
happy for a while, and that was nice. My little brother and
I were happy, too, because there was an upstairs and a
garden. Perfect. It was a good day and it was just about to
get a little better.

Eddie and Pauline lived just around the corner. That was
a real result for us, as they were brilliant. They could pop
in for a cuppa whenever they wanted to. Great.

Martha, as I said, had been seeing the Irish beefcake,
Kevin Shaunessy, and they had an announcement to make.
They were going to get married. That surprised us all—
especially Dad. Anyway, he soon realised that it didn't
matter what he said— they would get married anyway. So
he gave them their blessing, and they were married. She was
eighteen.

For the next few months I was just letting people know
that I was leaving. The new school I would go to would be
Wheelers Lane School in Kings Heath. My cousin Martin
went to Kings Heath, but I had already made a few friends
and they went to Wheelers Lane, so it was decided.

My old friends in Pleasant Park were being left behind,
and thankfully I was moving south and not north, because I
thought it might be warmer, so south I was pleased with.
When we finally moved in April, I was ready to go. I had
said all my goodbyes and I felt it was time. We gathered
whatever few things we had and away we went. As soon as
I got to the new house, it was a relief. I quickly settled in
my new bedroom and organised an old record player so I
could spin some tunes. A room to myself and a record
player— things had certainly changed and for the best. The
next few days I looked around the neighbourhood and made
friends with some neighbours. Mark Hart was one of them.
He was a tall, blond-headed lad who was a good looking kid

with a great personality. He looked like a lanky Harpo Marx. I think we hit it off immediately. He liked something about me and I liked something about him. Thirty years later we are still trying to work it out. In those first few tentative weeks Mark, who was a popular lad, would introduce me to people who would drag me through my years in Billesley. Football was always on the menu. I wasn't brilliant, but I had a big heart. I would play football continuously that summer, and Dad did kick the habit of his sleeping pills. However, he could not kick the booze and it would take over now and then, but overall the move to Billesley was positive. In my first year at school I would meet people who would have a great influence on me. Paul Titley was a good friend who lived locally, and we became inseparable, as I did with Mickey Seeney. I stopped wetting the bed, too. It's nice to wake up dry— I fully recommend it.

The scars of what happened in Pleasant Park healed a little, but my closest friends, when they looked hard enough, still saw a frightened little boy trying to fit in. Sometimes he tried too hard and sometimes he tried to little, but at least he tried.

Epilogue

IN WRITING THIS BOOK, I REALISED WHAT THE ANSWER to my question— when sitting on my bedroom windowsill and asking myself what the meaning of my life was— is. Of course, the answer is now simple: the birth of my son and the writing of this book. I have met many wonderful and truly amazing people along the way to doing these things.

Meeting these people and having them as part of my life has helped me in my eventual quest of telling my story. If this story helps just one person cope with any hardship, anything at all, related to this book, then that is all I ask for. One person in particular gave me feedback during the course of this book, and he said that it made him laugh, made him cry and made him think.

As a writer, that is all I can wish for. If you are reading this book and paid money for it, I thank you for that, and I hope you enjoyed the story. I hope it made you laugh, made you cry, and made you think.

Regards,
Christian